FROM
HOLYWOOD
TO
HOLLYWOOD

Paul Tweed is an internationally recognised expert in the field of media law and reputation management. Having been described as 'the most powerful man in Hollywood', Paul has represented governments, corporations and A-List celebrities such as Sinéad O'Connor, Liam Neeson, Sylvester Stallone, Arnold Schwarzenegger, Justin Timberlake, Louis Walsh, Johnny Depp and Amber Heard.

FROM
HOLYWOOD
TO
HOLLYWOOD

*My Life as an International Libel Lawyer
to the Rich and Famous*

PAUL TWEED

MERRION
PRESS

First published in 2024 by
Merrion Press
10 George's Street
Newbridge
Co. Kildare
Ireland
www.merrionpress.ie

9781785375217 (Paper)
9781785375323 (Ebook)

A CIP catalogue record for this book is
available from the British Library.

Typeset in Sabon LT Std 11.5/17 pt

Cover design: Padraig McCormack
Front and back cover photographs: Khara Pringle

Merrion Press is a member of Publishing Ireland

Dedicated to Selena,
my wife and partner in law

CONTENTS

INTRODUCTION

I had thought of writing a book for some years, in part prompted by friends and clients suggesting the idea to me. I have been fortunate to have had a varied and interesting career that has taken me all over the world, giving me the opportunity to work for everyone from A-list celebrities and musicians to members of the judiciary and journalists. What has finally encouraged me put pen to paper, though, are the extraordinary developments in Big Tech – and especially in artificial intelligence (AI) – that I have come to realise pose a threat to all of us, our younger generation in particular. I therefore hope that this book will highlight the global and societal challenges facing lawyers like myself. Legislation lags far behind these developments and continues to do so. I hope that this book will show how we can learn from past mistakes, and that it might also jolt the traditional media into action, and indeed all of us.

Over the past four decades, I have had the privilege and professional challenge of acting for a broad range of clients. As well as the film stars and musicians, I have worked on behalf of politicians across the religious and political divides, and for many newspapers, publishers and journalists (the latter still make up the largest group of clients who regularly consult me). I have also acted for many of my colleagues in the legal profession, which I have always regarded as the ultimate compliment.

Although I am restricted in what I can say for client confidentiality reasons, I have nonetheless received great support and help from many clients in the writing of this book. I am also very grateful to those journalists and authors who have not only supported and encouraged me in my career but who have provided invaluable guidance for dealing with an ever-changing media landscape.

It would be impossible to get into the detail of all the issues that Big Tech throws up. However, in relating my own professional and personal challenges, and my work on behalf of clients, I hope I have made clear how difficult and expensive it is to obtain justice in this area. Perhaps this knowledge might even act as a lightning rod to encourage others to join the online battle.

Part of my story is about attempts to neuter me, or throw my career off track. As a lawyer, I am really not expecting any sympathy, but I do want to make the point that it is not all one-way traffic. Media lawyers are often portrayed as the agent provocateurs and the primary threat to freedom of speech. On the contrary, not only is it a two-way street, but lawyers are very often the protectors of accurate speech and of the credibility of investigative journalism, which itself is at risk of being destroyed by developments in AI.

Since I began working as a lawyer some forty years ago in and around the small town of Holywood in Northern

Ireland, I have witnessed seismic changes in the legal world
that I could not have foreseen, never mind anticipated.
And my career has developed in a totally unexpected way
– even in my wildest dreams, I did not imagine a client list
that would take me all the way to the other Hollywood
in California, the Middle East and beyond. At the outset
of my career, my main worry had been that I would be
bored. I did not for a moment anticipate that one day I
would spend my time mixing with celebrities and powerful
entrepreneurs, and what I definitely could not have
imagined was that my daily routine would be interrupted
as a result of being followed by private investigators who
had been retained on behalf of a hostile state, or being
subjected to attempts to hack into my iPhone and IT
systems by anonymous bad actors. I have also been the
focus of malicious and targeted disinformation campaigns
orchestrated by disgruntled opponents. The concern is
that if these people are prepared to attack me, with my
perceived expertise in this field, what chance do the general
public have in dealing with similar issues?

So the image of a lawyer sitting behind a desk, working
through a pile of files, making phone calls and occasionally
appearing in court is now a quaint anachronism.
Nowadays, 'a day in the office' is rarely spent in the
office, and wherever I am, there is no guarantee of respite
from the cyber and other subterfuge that is a common
feature in 'global lawfare'. Even the numerous attempts
over the years by defendants hoping to find dirt on me
by having me followed by private investigators is like a

memory from a 1960s TV show. I can remember getting feedback from a journalist client conveying their superior's frustration that all the investigators' reports came back with the same theme: that I appeared to do nothing but work, no matter what day of the week or hour of the day or night they followed me. In one sense I was glad to have the reputation as a hard worker; on the other hand, it was slightly disappointing to be portrayed as having a somewhat boring existence and lifestyle!

I have always enjoyed the 'hunt', and when I get my teeth into a case, I find the hours rapidly turning into days, while I try to outmanoeuvre and outsmart my opponents. Over the years I have undoubtedly done some of my best work between the hours of 5 a.m. and 7 a.m., or on a Friday evening, or over a weekend, when many of my colleagues are either in a restaurant or on the golf course. No doubt they are the smarter ones in that they have a more varied and relaxing lifestyle, not to mention actually having a life outside work. However, I have never lost the drive and commitment that I had when I first entered the profession, turning my attention from criminal injury claims arising from the Troubles to building up a substantial insurance practice, and all the time gearing up to what would be my ultimate calling as an international media lawyer.

I have, rightly or wrongly, believed that my limited qualities – or character flaws, depending on your viewpoint – have worked to my advantage, no matter what the geographical location or client interests involved. I have always tried to learn from my mistakes and not make them again – not something all my adversaries have done, as you will pick up in the following chapters. My mother always did worry about my inability to forgive and forget until I have got even. While this may not be a laudable trait, I am absolutely convinced that it is something that has set me up well for dealing with people who have sought to undermine me by using underhand or unfair tactics.

When I set out as a lawyer in the late 1970s, we were living in very challenging and uncertain times in Belfast. The legal system had to withstand the intense pressures placed on it by the civil strife and turbulence of that troubled period. Life went on nevertheless, and we all had to adapt to the circumstances and carry on regardless. That being said, there have been occasions when I felt the need to check under my car before letting my children get in, if only to satisfy my own paranoia at any particular time. However, I was fortunate in that I was not personally exposed to the worst excesses of the violence, while at the same time acting for clients from either side of the political fence, an approach I have always maintained. I may be naïve in saying this, but I have always felt that most of my clients have shown the same degree of loyalty to me as I have shown to them over the years. Whether I'm working in Northern Ireland or in the Middle East, in my world trust is everything, and is vital to the running of any high-profile legal action.

In the past, I always had the utmost respect for my adversaries, who were most often newspapers or publishers (with me sometimes acting for and sometimes acting against them). I am now facing much more powerful, global and usually faceless opponents in the form of Google/YouTube, Meta/Facebook/Instagram, X/Twitter and their equivalent AI platforms and chatbots. The threat of a substantial damages award and significant legal costs, never mind a handful of determined lawyers, holds no fear or concern for them.

I will have achieved what I set out to do if I manage to encourage the next generation of lawyers to follow their ambition and have belief in themselves. I hope the book will also give hope to anyone who has been the victim of a disinformation campaign, or harassment, abuse or bullying on social media. In modern times, defamation of character often takes second place to a misuse of private information and data breaches. Indeed, privacy and personal data have one thing in common – like that other precious commodity water, once it has evaporated, it is impossible to get it back. While we have always valued and jealously guarded our reputations and privacy, our data has suddenly become an even more vulnerable resource, with enormous commercial importance to those who have possession of it. Not only does it represent a valuable asset, but it is also a potential means of controlling our lives. This provides an obvious explanation as to why a number of the online giants have made it their business to attempt to transfer data from this side of the Atlantic over to what they perceive as the safe haven of the United States (US), with their First Amendment and other protections, which are much more in favour of a publisher.

In the grander scheme of things, it is essential to be creative and be as innovative as those conglomerates on the other side of the fence. I have never shied away from a good fight, and while the story of David and Goliath springs to mind, my colleagues and I will have more than a slingshot at our disposal. I suppose there will be a day when I stop to ask myself what was I doing all this for and what have I achieved. But even at my stage in life I have yet to reach that point, and I have no intention of stopping to find out any time soon. In fact, the dramatic increase in pace online suits my style and way of working. It just means that the adrenaline flows that bit faster.

Let the battle continue!

ONE

Uncertain Beginnings

My story begins in 1952, before I was even born, when a jury sitting at the Crumlin Road courthouse in Belfast announced its verdict. They had heard the highly emotional testimony of a young legal secretary, along with the evidence of her father and her fiancé, and had found in their favour. The court awarded damages of £250 to the plaintiffs, finding that they had been slandered by a member of the legal secretary's fiancé's family. The plaintiffs were my mother, Betty Loudon, and her father, Martin.

The case came about after my parents had become engaged. My father's wealthy Aunt Mary had offered to fund the deposit on his and my mother's first home, which was £250, a significant sum back in those days. However, other members of my father's extended family interfered – they disapproved of the engagement because my mother came from a working-class background – and persuaded Aunt Mary to withdraw her generous gift, even though my parents had already had their offer on a property accepted and needed the deposit. If this was not bad enough, Aunt

Mary had also vindictively repeated hurtful and false allegations about my mother and her father, which resulted in them suing her for slander. So far as I am aware, taking libel – never mind slander – proceedings back in the day was very unusual, especially for ordinary people, as well as being risky and stressful.

The £250 awarded to my parents was hardly the £1 million in libel damages that the publishers of *The Sun* newspaper paid out to Sir Elton John in 1988 over a series of false stories, or the $15 million awarded to Johnny Depp by a jury in his US defamation suit against his former wife, Amber Heard. Nonetheless it was a significant sum for a young couple back in those days, even if it came too late for them to buy the home they had set their hearts on.

I did not know about any of this until shortly before my mother passed away, but I now view it as prescient serendipity, given my subsequent career as a media lawyer. I don't know why my parents never talked about it, but their relationship with Aunt Mary definitely improved over the years, as we were often taken to visit her when we were children.

My father had had what must have been a difficult and unusual childhood in that he was handed over by his parents around the age of three to his Aunt Mary and his grandmother, for reasons that were unknown to us; they effectively reared him, within four or five miles of his parents' farm. He went on to become a bank manager at the Trustee Savings Bank (TSB). Maybe it was just the way things were in the 1960s, but none of this was ever discussed with me or my two brothers.

Growing up in the seaside town of Bangor, County Down, my primary interest in life was sport. Anything involving a ball and some form of competition appealed to me, and, when I wasn't at school, I was out on the street or in one of the fields near our house from dawn to dusk. I saw school as nothing more than a necessary means to an end.

I passed the eleven-plus exam and went on to Bangor Grammar School in 1966, but I wasn't particularly studious or academic. At school, my focus was on rugby and tennis, and I seized every opportunity to play football in my spare time. As I approached my university years, squash became my main passion. Although I never had a particular talent for any of these sports, I loved anything involving intense physical activity. This led me to participate in the first Newtownards marathon, with minimal preparation – my limited training involved a maximum distance of about ten miles. On the day of the race, I made it to the finishing line in four hours and twenty minutes, notwithstanding my lack of training, inappropriate running shoes and sportswear, albeit with blood coming from my chest and toes, much to the bewilderment and concern of those watching.

The following year, I adopted a much more sensible approach in preparing for the inaugural Belfast marathon and did some proper training with several friends, including fellow law student and Swindon and Linfield football player, Peter Dornan. While I couldn't possibly compete with Peter's level of fitness, it was a help to me that Peter never took anything particularly seriously, and we had some fun overtaking each other during the first twenty miles or so. However, it all became much more competitive in the final mile. I still think in amusement of us crossing the line together, wrestling with one another in our efforts to finish ahead!

As I entered my final year at school, I had no idea what I wanted to do. My mother was very keen for me to go to university to study law. She became so frustrated at my apparent lack of direction that she gave me an ultimatum: if I didn't follow her preferred route, then I had to look for a job in the civil service or a bank. I applied to study law at a number of universities. Having scraped through my A levels, I was fortunate to receive one – and only one – offer, and that was from Queen's University Belfast. When I enrolled in 1973, I had not developed the work ethic for which I am now known, and only attended lectures when there was no one to cover for me and no other option. I never really had any interest in university life, probably due to the fact that I chose to live at home rather than staying in university accommodation. Costs were a major consideration, even though I was in receipt of the maximum grant. I did make some good friends, however. While hard work did not come naturally to me at university, I supplemented my grant with income from holiday jobs – working as a postman during the Christmas break, at a bar polishing tables at Easter, and then, in the summers, at Pritchitts, a local ice cream factory that, back in the 1970s, paid what seemed like enormous wages to students who were prepared to work every available hour of overtime.

Notwithstanding my father's seemingly grand title of 'bank manager', this was not reflected in his earnings from the TSB. Apart from a discounted mortgage, his pay was comparatively modest, to the extent that my mother's allowance for the groceries and other household expenses was almost all spent on payday in discharging the monthly bills. She then had to face the challenge of surviving financially for the rest of the month. I remember being sent to the local shop to purchase a single cigarette on frequent occasions. This precarious background may go some way to explaining my drive for financial security throughout my career, even though I have never been remotely motivated by the actual spending of money.

After four years at Queen's, I managed to graduate with an honours degree. I was admitted to the Institute of Legal Studies, where I studied for a year. I then needed to find a firm to employ me for two years of restricted practising in order to become a fully qualified solicitor. By this stage, I had run up an overdraft in excess of £13,000, with no idea (or thought) as to how and when I would be able to pay it off. However, even back in those days I had absolute confidence in myself and my ability to achieve anything I set my heart on.

I eventually landed an offer from Herbie McCracken, a senior partner in Johnsons Solicitors, primarily a property and corporate law firm based in Belfast. I started on an annual salary of £2,500 and tried to forget about the overdraft. I continued to believe that everything comes good in the end. At the time, I had no intention of staying more than two years with the firm, but even that period felt as if it was going to be too long for me.

After a couple of months I began applying for jobs, driven by a combination of impatience, naivety and misplaced self-confidence. The positions ranged from the governor of the Solomon Islands to an intellectual property lawyer with the drinks conglomerate Distillers. I had no experience, no expertise and no idea what the jobs entailed. Needless to say, these two applications were not successful, but I did manage to get an interview in London with the senior partner at W.S. Walker & Co., a Cayman Islands-based corporate law firm. I think he must have decided to meet me out of astonishment at my brass neck, but we had an excellent lunch and a very interesting discussion. The trip itself was a major treat for me in those days. I was not, of course, offered a job in the end.

What I did learn during these early stages of my career was that the practice of law is made up of many different aspects and types of work. While a number of my contemporaries were more than happy to practise property and corporate law, and were interested in that field, it just had no appeal for me, not least because it seemed to be entirely office-based and a bit mundane. Then some of my friends started to tell me about the high-volume insurance work they were doing. As well as getting a certain buzz from the court appearances and negotiation sessions, they were also earning more money, for their firms and for themselves. Good fortune had it that the firm received an introduction to Guardian Insurance (now AXA) through Bob McCartney, a leading senior counsel and good friend of Herbie McCracken. Before long, I had a solid understanding of how to attract more of this type of work. The first step was to establish a good personal relationship with the claims manager and the support team in order to get the opportunity to show what we could do and, equally importantly, that we could do it in a manner that suited their particular policy aims. These strategic objectives were not the same for each insurer. Some firms adopted a policy of settling as early and quickly as possible, even if this meant paying more in terms of damages in order to save on legal costs. Other companies preferred to put up a robust fight in the belief that this would discourage other claims and result in better settlements in the long term.

The claims we were instructed to process tended to be road traffic accident or employer's liability claims. As claims can take some time, insurers need to know how much to set aside from their funds for each claim – and part of our job was to provide an estimate of this financial exposure, known as a reserve. Once the insurer knows the reserve, it can decide how to proceed and whether or not to settle.

With the strong work ethic and unflinching support of another partner, John Marshall, I managed to bring more than a dozen insurance companies to Johnsons during the 1980s, and had a bit of craic in doing so. I concentrated on employer's liability, personal injury, product liability and professional indemnity claims, all of which were much easier to handle on the defence side than the greater uncertainty of plaintiff litigation.

In tandem with this work, I gradually built up quite a substantial criminal injury practice, work which came about as a direct result of the Troubles. I developed considerable sympathy for the soldiers I represented. Some of them had suffered the most horrendous injuries and, until we became involved, had received minimal compensation from the Northern Ireland Office. Most – if not all – of these claims had been processed within the Army circle, and the soldiers were expected to accept the first offer that was put on the table – almost as if it was their duty. Although these claims did not pay particularly well in terms of legal costs because of a very tight statutory scale, the sheer volume compensated to some degree. Our firm acted for non-military personnel as well, often for people who had been caught in a bomb explosion or who had been the victims of a random sectarian attack on either side of the religious and political divide.

The Troubles of course also impacted on the legal profession – judges were regarded as targets and several high-profile solicitors also lost their lives. With our office being in Belfast city centre, we became used to evacuations because of bomb scares and explosions. Even getting into work could be difficult, and taking the train presented its own particular challenges. During my student days, a bomb was found in the carriage I had been travelling in on my commute to Queen's! Like everyone else, we had no choice but to get on with life, and gradually we developed a resilience to the chaos that was going on around us.

Indeed, the everyday trauma faced by many in the legal profession provided us with a strong backbone for dealing with the more subtle challenges of the modern era. Whether it be verbal threats or not so subtle surveillance, it would take significant intimidation to come close to some of my past experiences. As David Ervine, the late Progressive Unionist Party (PUP) politician and former prisoner once remarked to me, 'If you are told of the threat, you can normally take it that it is no more than that. The genuine threat usually becomes known when it is too late!'

A positive outcome was that a particularly tough and resilient legal profession emerged, hardened by the chaos around us. The challenges we faced every day made any 'see you in court' type threats from opposing lawyers laughable.

TWO

Buns and Boxing

Although business was good, I don't think I could have put up with the day-to-day working life of a personal injury litigator for ever. Fortunately for me, a case came along that changed everything. In 1986 the *Sunday World* published a story claiming that two leading Belfast QCs, Bob McCartney and Des Boal, had fought over the last chocolate éclair in a cake shop in Holywood, County Down.

I had been contacted by Bob on the day after the paper had appeared on the newsstands, and he was not happy. He immediately dictated a robust letter of complaint that he wanted me to deliver by hand to the editor, such was his determination to deal with this fabricated story.

Bob had become a mentor to me in the early stages of my career as a litigator. To describe him as one of the most successful and feared senior counsel of his era only gives part of the picture. Bob was a force of nature who took control of his cases from the outset and was fearless in his determination to get a result. This approach was also evident when he was sitting on the other side of the fence as a client, as in this case – such was the intensity of his involvement in the litigation strategy that it was easy to forget that he was not actually the counsel directing the legal proceedings.

This case could have been settled quickly with an appropriate apology from the newspaper, but instead, those behind the *Sunday World* adopted a provocative stance. The condescending attitude of their lawyers didn't help – it would have been a big mistake to treat Bob in this way at any time, but it was disastrous for them in a personal matter that he was taking very seriously. Following an intense exchange of correspondence with the *Sunday World's* lawyers and the rapid processing of the legal action, we found ourselves at the door of the court in no time at all, at least in comparison to similar defamation actions. To say that Bob was full-on and determined to achieve a result quickly is a considerable understatement. However not so his co-plaintiff. Although Des Boal was regarded as one of the most aggressive and ruthless criminal silks of his day, his enthusiasm for his own case seemed a bit muted. He did however hang in with Bob, albeit contributing the bare minimum to our preparations, despite encouragement from his own legal team. It all culminated in a viciously fought case, lasting a number of days, at the end of which the plaintiffs were awarded £50,000 each.

To some, this complaint might seem trivial. However, a leading counsel should have not only an impeccable reputation but also a formidable one. The *Sunday World* story was a deliberate attempt to undermine Bob's hard-earned reputation as a serious and extremely effective advocate. A defamation case is based on the fundamental premise that the story has undermined a person's character in the eyes of the general public. The cream bun story – notwithstanding the apparently trite subject matter – was a prime example of the impact of ridicule, which it turned out had been supplied to the paper by a jealous begrudger, who was also a lawyer.

The awards of £50,000 each to Bob and to Des Boal might also sound excessive to anyone who did not have the benefit of hearing Bob McCartney give his evidence describing the impact of the story on him, both professionally and personally. The seven local people who made up the jury could clearly relate to his concerns as a self-made working-class man.

Since the introduction of the 2013 Defamation Act in England, under English law, claimants must show that what has been written about them has caused 'serious harm'. Bob McCartney's and Des Boal's action would have been an interesting test case if this legislation had been in place then. In my view, the Belfast jury must have come to an unequivocal conclusion that there was serious harm, hence the substantial damages awarded.

While I can take little or no credit for the successful outcome of this landmark case – which was primarily due to the brilliance and determination of Bob McCartney, and the input of our counsel – it did whet my appetite and open up a whole new world to me.

I was very fortunate to have Bob take me under his wing at such an early stage in my career, at a time when a number of charismatic and exceptionally talented counsel came to the fore. Whether it was due to the difficult circumstances caused by the Troubles or just coincidence, the likes of Bob, Brian Kerr, John Gillen, Ben Stephens and David Ringland were in a league of their own. Bob McCartney was not only an inspiration, but he also introduced me to another larger-than-life character, the renowned businessman, bookmaker and boxing promoter Barney Eastwood, known to his family and friends as BJ. This initial introduction led to me to representing BJ Eastwood for the next thirty years, and to one of the most talked-about and dramatic defamation actions for a generation.

Barney Eastwood was a well-known figure in Northern Ireland and beyond. By the late 1950s, he was running small boxing shows in Belfast, and soon he was managing the careers of individual boxers, many of whom became world champions. At the same time, his bookmaking and business empire was flourishing – ultimately, in 2008, he sold his fifty-four betting shops to Ladbrokes in a deal worth £135 million. A prodigiously hard worker with exceptional instincts, BJ Eastwood had a reputation as a brilliant and formidable adversary, and an extremely talented boxing manager and promoter. At one point, he had five world champions on his books, at the same time as he was running an extensive bookmaking business and property empire.

During this period, very few promoters were prepared to bring performers of any ilk to Belfast because of the Troubles. It was left to boxing promoters like BJ to fill the entertainment void by bringing championship bouts to the King's Hall. In fact, BJ often had to boost the promotion with fighters from his own stable, such was the lack of enthusiasm from overseas promoters.

The most famous boxer BJ managed was Barry McGuigan. McGuigan achieved international renown in June 1985 when he became World Boxing Association (WBA) Featherweight Champion after defeating the defending title holder, Eusebio Pedroza, at Loftus Road in London. From Clones in the Irish Republic, but representing both Northern Ireland and the Republic in various international boxing contests, McGuigan was already a national hero by the mid-eighties. His World Featherweight win intensified his fans' adulation, and he came home to a hero's welcome, when over 75,000 people packed the streets of Belfast to celebrate his victory. In a Northern Ireland beset by turmoil and tragedy, McGuigan's success was all the more celebrated. His deliberately non-partisan stance seemed like a beacon of hope. As someone who had drawn the world's attention to Northern Ireland for reasons other than sectarian hatred and murder, the 'Clones Cyclone' was adored and revered.

BJ had guided his prodigy to his great victory at Loftus Road, but not long after, the honeymoon was over. The very substantial financial investment that BJ had put into the early fights, the many words of grateful thanks Barry had publicly given to his manager – which even became the basis of a hit song by comedian Dermot Morgan, 'Thank you very much, Mr. Eastwood' – were all forgotten. This catalyst for everything turning sour was McGuigan's unexpected defeat to a total outsider, Steve Cruz, in June 1986. The Argentinian boxer, Fernando Sosa, should have been McGuigan's opponent for the title defence, but Sosa had had to withdraw because of a detached retina. McGuigan was given the option of fighting Cruz, an unheralded 'part-timer' opponent from Fort Worth in Texas in Las Vegas, or a more experienced and difficult opponent, but in a better climate away from the heat of Sin City. A decision to fight Cruz was taken in conjunction with the boxer, but unfortunately McGuigan lost his World Title to this underdog, leading to bitter recriminations and a plethora of lawsuits.

The initial litigation focused primarily on McGuigan's complaint that his former manager should not also have been acting as the promoter of his fights. A manager, in return for a percentage of the purse (normally up to 25 per cent), was obliged to look after the boxer's interests. McGuigan argued that this was incompatible with the manager also acting as a promoter and staging the fight, making an additional profit. However, as I have already explained, BJ had really no option but to promote his own fights as nobody else was coming forward to do so. In fact, he lost money on at least the first ten McGuigan fights.

Ironically, some thirty years later, McGuigan – having entered boxing management after the end of his own career – was sued by one of his boxers, Carl Frampton, for *acting as both manager and promoter*, among other complaints. I couldn't believe it when I first read those headlines!

Subsequent litigation developed with McGuigan claiming BJ had put him into the ring when he was injured. When McGuigan repeated this allegation in a documentary produced by Channel 5 Video Distribution Ltd, a PolyGram subsidiary, BJ contacted me for advice in relation to the legal options available to him. After due consideration, we dispatched a robust letter of complaint to McGuigan and Channel 5 Video, leaving them in no doubt as to BJ's outrage regarding the defamatory allegation. However, with no satisfactory reply forthcoming, we were left with little alternative but to arrange for the issue of defamation proceedings in the High Court in Belfast, against both McGuigan and Channel 5 Video Distribution, albeit with cautious reservations being expressed by counsel.

Unlike many of the modern-day defamation actions that begin with argument over the meanings of the words used in the alleged libel, the sting in this case was clear cut: that BJ had forced McGuigan to fight with an injured ankle. Obviously medical evidence and the testimony of those closely involved in the preparations for the contest would be highly significant, if not crucial.

The legal action turned out to be a World Title contest in its own right. Although the burden of proof rested on the defendants – they had to prove the veracity of the defamatory allegation – BJ and I nonetheless travelled the length and breadth of the US to interview potential witnesses. These ranged from sparring partners and physiotherapists to the referee and ringside officials, whom we believed would support BJ's absolute repudiation of the boxer's defamatory allegation. Many of these witnesses agreed to travel to Belfast for the hearing and it was an interesting learning curve for me to meet participants from the ground up in the world of international boxing.

Fortunately, even though the trial was taking place some years after the actual championship bout, most of those we spoke to had clear and lucid memories of the events leading up to the fight, and were adamant that McGuigan had not been injured before entering the ring. These witnesses included the physiotherapist for the LA Lakers basketball team, who had treated McGuigan in the run-up to the fight; the referee and two of the ringside judges; and one of his sparring partners, Jeff Franklin. Franklin explained in graphic terms just how fit McGuigan was for the fight: McGuigan had given him a severe trouncing in the ring just days beforehand, much to the chagrin of Franklin, who had brought his girlfriend down to Vegas to watch the warm-up bout. Another key witness for us turned out to be the fight referee, Richard Steele, a tough, no-nonsense raconteur, who made it absolutely clear that if McGuigan had been injured, it would have been obvious to the referee from the opening bell.

Unknown to us, the other side were conducting precisely the same exercise. However, even if we had known, we would not have been particularly concerned because we had absolute confidence in the people we had interviewed. In the Irish jurisdictions, unlike in many other countries, you do not have to inform your opponents or the court in advance as to the identity of the witnesses you are intending to call. This enables the parties to catch their opponents off guard and retain an element of surprise. In the Eastwood case, we all took this potential to extremes. Both sides produced unexpected witnesses day by day, increasing the tension and leading to a rollercoaster of a case.

Given the fact that our pre-trial investigations confirmed, beyond any shadow of a doubt, BJ's account of events, we could not understand the apparent confidence in McGuigan's camp before the case kicked off. BJ had put forward a final offer the night before to settle the case if McGuigan apologised and made a donation to the Royal Victoria Hospital Intensive Care Unit where one of the Eastwoods' children had been treated before his tragic death the previous year. This was not only rejected, but McGuigan's solicitor, Eamonn McEvoy, did what we later referred to as a 'dervish dance' in apparent celebration at his client's refusal to accept what we had regarded as a magnanimous offer.

We finally understood their confidence – albeit misplaced – when they opened their case by calling as a witness a doctor from an LA hospital, whom we had not been able to track down. This Dr Johnston gave evidence that he had treated an injury sustained by McGuigan a number of days before the fight, much to BJ's bewilderment. Even though we did not understand or accept this, it would take several weeks of evidence from other witnesses before the case began to turn in BJ's favour.

Although BJ and I had spent many evenings at his home discussing potential sources of evidence and strategic options, we couldn't have predicted the drama of each day of the five-week hearing, especially the mornings when an unexpected witness was called to the box, requiring on-the-spot preparations for cross-examination. We did, of course, have a major advantage in the stellar advocacy and other skills of our counsel, Bob McCartney and Ben Stephens. Another key factor was McGuigan's own recently published autobiography, which came back to haunt him in the witness box. Time and again, our counsel were able to cite paragraphs that blatantly contradicted statements Mr McGuigan had made in the witness box.

BJ and I were very much in the minority in our confidence in the case. Most members of the local legal profession and the public seemed sure that local hero McGuigan's charm and personality would carry the day for him. Indeed, a neighbour of mine, who was a judge, called at my home during the trial to say he was worried that I was putting my neck and reputation on the line at a very young age, and that we could not possibly win.

However, the members of the jury heard all the evidence first hand and were in a position to assess the credibility of each witness as they shared stories and opinions in the witness box. This applied especially when it was time for BJ and McGuigan to take their respective turns to give their versions of events. Even though the witness list included a 'who's who' of the fight game, along with many respected medical experts, ring officials and boxing commentators, it was the evidence of the two protagonists that gripped the attention of the outside world.

When it comes to the time for a plaintiff or a defendant or any witness to give their evidence before the court, that person is not allowed to engage or speak with anyone else until discharged by the judge. To do so is a contempt of court and a potential disciplinary matter if a lawyer is involved. BJ's session in the witness box lasted several days, and he remarked after the hearing that he felt like a leper for not being able to talk to anybody during this period. As had been our habit during the case, Bob and I headed to nearby Bittle's Bar for lunch, and whilst sitting at our table, Bob noticed a familiar face in the mirror behind the bar. We both recognised him as a local private investigator, who had clearly been tasked with keeping an eye on us to ensure that we did not talk to our client. While we would not have dreamed of doing so, we regarded this as a clear indication of the mindset of McGuigan's solicitor, Eamonn McEvoy, and it took considerable restraint for us not to go over to the investigator and tell him what we thought about him and McEvoy!

The jury members' faces gave little away as they retired to consider their verdict, but when they came back, it was to deliver a resounding and dramatic award in BJ Eastwood's favour. The announcement produced whoops of joy and loud shouts from the public gallery, in contrast to the stony silence and grave looks from the McGuigan camp. Such was the uproar that the judge had to bang his gavel, demanding silence. The record damages of £450,000 awarded by these seven men and women, after a five-week hearing, had particular significance. It was not dissimilar to my mother's slander case in that the figure represented a financial marker allegedly agreed between the parties, in this case prior to the Las Vegas fight and which had been the subject of intense debate before and during the proceedings. This had been an amount that BJ had allegedly agreed to pay McGuigan as part of the financial agreement, in addition to the boxer's proportion of the purse, and it had been thrown into the background of the legal proceedings for the jury's consideration.

After the announcement of the verdict, we made our way past the media scrum and ended up in nearby Rumpole's bar. We had just popped the cork on the first bottle of champagne when we noticed members of the jury sitting in a booth close to our table. One of our number made his way over to say thank you to them, but before he had even reached their table, never mind opened his mouth to speak, there was an enormous barrage of camera flashbulbs going off from the other side of the window. The next day, *The Sun* newspaper carried a front-page story suggesting that BJ and his legal team were seen entertaining the jurors. This was another lesson for me – this time in the importance of avoiding situations that could be misinterpreted, and the importance of making sure I can anticipate what is likely to appear in the press so far as possible.

If the 'Cream Bun' case had been a gruelling initiation into the high-octane world of defamation litigation, the Eastwood and McGuigan legal battle was the ultimate baptism of fire. It evolved into the most sensational libel action in Irish legal history – in terms of the record damages awarded, its duration, the witnesses from as far afield as Las Vegas and LA, and the level of media interest it attracted. It was also exceptional because of the unprecedented level of vitriol that characterised the exchanges between my opposite number and me, and to a lesser degree, between counsel for the opposing parties. A judge who was presiding over one of the preliminary applications remarked at one point that the correspondence between McGuigan's solicitor and myself contained potentially more defamatory material than the subject allegations!

Such an acrimonious hearing is a relatively rare occurrence, especially since very few defamation cases ever get as far as the courts. In the world of libel litigation, a courtroom confrontation of this kind is a worst-case scenario and something which most media lawyers will do their level best to avoid by exploring as many avenues as possible for achieving an out-of-court settlement. Anyone who has had first-hand experience of how taxing a trial can be, both physically and emotionally, will understand why.

However, Eamonn McEvoy – whom I found to be particularly odious towards me personally and a very bad loser – had been aggressive and uncompromising from the word go, in effect ruling out any possibility of a negotiated, never mind amicable, settlement. This was unfortunate – and very bad news for his client. Our team could not help but get the feeling that it was McEvoy driving the litigation, rather than McGuigan, like a compulsive gambler believing that this was the one that he could win, despite having already lost multiple cases against Eastwood in the High Court and before the British Boxing Board of Control – a prime example of someone 'boxing above their weight' and refusing to learn from past mistakes and experiences.

The *Sunday Tribune* had described the case as 'the Undisputed Libel Championship of the World', and after the case BJ presented me with a beautiful cut-glass bowl, engraved with the words, '*To Paul "the Hitman" Tweed, the Undisputed Champion of the Law Courts. From BJ, Frances and All the Eastwood Family*'. The bowl has pride of place in my home office, and to this day, despite acting for many A-list celebrities, global entrepreneurs and famous political figures in hard-fought disputes, I still regard the Eastwood case as my biggest challenge and success. It turned out to be the starting gun for the beginnings of an unlikely global legal practice for me. The drama and the publicity surrounding the case got into my veins and gave me an adrenaline rush that I haven't stopped chasing ever since. I also learned the value of seizing the moment in terms of getting publicity for the client, the case and my firm, having learned from BJ Eastwood, the master of this strategy. Initially, like many of my fellow solicitors, I had been reluctant, embarrassed even, to put my head above the parapet. BJ was having none of it and thrust me forward into the glare of media attention at every opportunity. This ranged from putting me beside the charismatic boxer Chris Eubank and his manager Barry Hearn at the signing of a fight contract to being photographed standing on aeroplane steps before boarding a transatlantic flight to take on the WBA.

I realised in due course that my profile would benefit my clients, most of whom are very keen to have their reputation restored by way of an appropriate apology with or without a court hearing, and to have that news disseminated as widely and quickly as possible. I also realised that there is only one very brief window in which this can happen – any media interest wanes in a matter of hours rather than days. Some clients, of course, want the opposite and it can be a much more difficult challenge to keep an outcome out of the press!

The truth is that some people can never be satisfied. I once negotiated an apology for defamation – hard won, because the libel complaint wasn't straightforward – in a national newspaper for a wealthy businessman. I thought this was a highly satisfactory outcome, but the businessman took umbrage that the apology appeared too close to the obituary section in the paper. I had to spend the next few days trying to persuade the editor to re-run the apology on another page. He did so in the end, but more out of respect for our long professional relationship than out of sympathy for the client.

For someone else, I achieved front-page national coverage that reported that the defendant had apologised to him in court by spinning the very limited wording conceded by the other side. However, the client still complained that the defendant hadn't gone so far as to say sorry in court ... sometimes you just cannot win!

The Eastwood case not only gave me an insider's view of the 'Big Fight' game, but in turn introduced me to other players in the boxing world, including promoters such as Don King and Frank Warren, and boxers like Chris Eubank and Joe Calzaghe. The financial arrangements behind the sport also inevitably led to more litigation, some in the courts and others before the British Boxing Board of Control (BBBofC) and the WBA. The former European Middleweight Champion, Herol Graham, and his then manager, Brendan Ingle, became adversaries of BJ Eastwood back in the day, leading to a particularly vitriolic battle in front of the BBBofC, which at the time was chaired by 'Nipper' Reid, the former police inspector who was credited with bringing the London gangsters the Krays to justice. Eamonn McEvoy popped up again, this time for Graham, but we not only won that battle comprehensively but also a hard-fought libel action against the publishers of the *News of the World*. The latter ultimately conceded during the discovery process that Graham had accepted a substantial five-figure sum to 'turn over' his former manager, Mr Eastwood.

This defamation hearing had opened before a Belfast jury. However, the other side put forward a settlement offer of over £100,000 just as the jury were beginning to get interested. BJ and I were left to speculate how much he would ultimately have been awarded if the action had been allowed to run its course. However, a 'bird in the hand' is always to be welcomed, and the case still provided good fodder for our many discussions in BJ's bar/snooker room at his home.

Unlike many of my clients over the years, BJ simply loved litigation. He appeared to treat it as an extension of his boxing promotions, with the resultant adrenaline rush. I often had considerable difficulty in persuading him to settle his many subsequent libel actions, thereby depriving him of his day in court.

I was fortunate to become involved in what was probably the end of a golden era in world boxing, with almost as much sparring going on between the various promoters, such as Mickey Duff, Jarvis Astaire, Bob Arum and Don King, as took place in the actual fight arena.

And I had a ringside seat!

THREE

What's Britney Got to Do with Belfast?

The adrenaline rush of these early libel actions gave me the incentive to completely change the direction of my legal practice from traditional litigation to media law and reputation management. The change was a slow process though, even with the success of these cases behind me.

It's very difficult to make defamation work pay for itself, particularly in Northern Ireland, where my media law practice was based in the early days. People tend to think a simple letter or phone call is all that is involved to resolve their issue, and that a couple of hundred pounds should be sufficient to cover my costs. In reality, for a letter or call to bring success, the other side has to be convinced that I am not bluffing and that I will drive the case into court if necessary. This requires not only careful and well-researched legal argument, but an innate knowledge of what is likely to be the most persuasive approach for that particular opponent based on my years of experience.

Even more importantly, any request or complaint made on behalf of a client will be strengthened by my own and my firm's track record of successfully contesting previous cases of a similar nature. I have spent countless hours and a professional lifetime building this reputation for striking quickly and effectively. Even with this in mind, though, I have been shocked at the legal costs recently proposed by colleagues representing the other side, especially in England. In one case, the defendants' solicitors estimated their fees in a relatively straightforward libel action to be in the region of an eyewatering £2.7 million. And this was after the English Defamation Act had been introduced in 2013 with a view to reducing legal costs!

Back to the 1990s, and with BJ Eastwood's libel actions beginning to multiply – with settlements ranging from £100,000 damages from the *News of the World* to £200,000 from the publisher Harper Collins – the contacts I made were primarily from the world of boxing and contractual negotiations. However, this was a different era, when gambling debts were often settled in kind, for instance with a painting from Lucien Freud or from other artists with a penchant for the odd bet. BJ was an avid art collector, and I accompanied him to a number of galleries and auctions, which in turn led to introductions to those involved in the art world and other very wealthy people. During this time, it was very clear to me that future business, or at least the work I hoped to attract, would be from outside the United Kingdom (UK) and Ireland. Although the fight game was more brutal than glamorous, as the changing rooms after a fight made clear, it was a good stepping stone and eye-opener for me.

I would eventually generate valuable publicity by getting results for celebrities and other people who were well known, but before then, I was dependent for new work on word of mouth and on introductions from well-placed clients. In the late nineties a barrister colleague recommended me to the legendary Northern Irish actor Liam Neeson, who had achieved incredible success in Hollywood movies. He was married to Natasha Richardson, who also had an eminently successful career, and who hailed from the famed acting dynasty. Her mother was Vanessa Redgrave, who also consulted me some years later.

In 1998 the *Daily Telegraph* had initiated a frenzy of inaccurate reporting with an article stating that Liam and Natasha had been seen leaving the offices of a well-known London divorce law firm. In fact, it was another member of the Richardson family who had been at that address, but before the *Telegraph* could publish a correction, the story was picked up across the UK and Irish media within a matter of hours. We managed to resolve most of the complaints against newspapers very quickly – the sensible publishers did the right thing on receipt of our legal correspondence. The publishers of the *Sunday Life*, however, decided to take a stand. We ended up before the Court of Appeal, with the Neesons having succeeded at every previous cut and turn. The Court of Appeal also found firmly in their favour, and the couple donated the damages they received to the victims of the August 1998 Omagh bomb explosion.

Acting for Liam and Natasha was in itself a marketing dream. I got on well with them from the outset and was enormously impressed with Liam's decisiveness and determination. I had frank phone conversations with him at each pivotal point in the litigation and ended up travelling to their New York apartment for consultations. Their response to my advice was always clear and unambiguous. They were the epitome of the Hollywood power couple, but they were totally unaffected by their incredible success. Liam lived up to his movie star persona and demonstrated remarkable backbone. I certainly wouldn't mess with him!

In the run-up to the new century another early breakthrough for my media law practice came when Philadelphia-based attorney Jimmy Binns approached me in relation to a false allegation published in one of the Irish papers. A story stated that he had been the 'bag man' for the WBA. Although Jimmy did act for the WBA, he took grave exception to this unfounded allegation. The newspaper was relatively prompt in accepting its mistake, and the matter was resolved without recourse to a court hearing. However, Jimmy's approach provided further encouragement to me in relation to the prospects for an international practice, not least due to the fact that he represented many high-profile celebrities himself. He had even played Rocky's lawyer in *Rocky V* and the Pennsylvania boxing commissioner in *Rocky Balboa*. At the end of the day, my work for Jimmy didn't result in other US-based clients coming to me at that stage, but it nonetheless made me even more aware of the opportunities in the USA.

I am often asked how 'someone from Belfast' has become the first port of call for many of the rich and famous when they have been defamed or their privacy invaded. I have sometimes asked myself that same question. So did the presenter of an ABC News broadcast in 2006, reporting on the case I had been handling for Britney Spears that had made the headlines. The reporter's curiosity was due not only to the profile of the famous claimant, but also because of where the legal exchanges were taking place. The documentary opened with scenes showing bomb explosions and riots – reflecting the international perception of Northern Ireland in a different time – and then displayed a map featuring a path from LA to Belfast, indicating surprise that a major US celebrity would be litigating in this part of the world. When I have replayed that ABC video at Law Society events, the reaction of a young lad on his bicycle when asked about the case and answering – 'What's Britney got to do with Belfast?' – always raises a resounding laugh. The prospect of international litigation in Belfast then was unimaginable for many, not least because many people hadn't realised that we were all hurtling towards a global internet era, with multi-jurisdictional implications. But before 2006 I had seen this opportunity coming and had spent several years criss-crossing the Atlantic in anticipation, not only establishing contacts, but gaining an understanding of the restrictions placed on US media litigants in their own country.

As regards my career in the USA, I will always be eternally grateful for the support and introductions I've received from one of the best media lawyers in the world, Marty Singer, with whom I became firm friends. Although Marty has the nickname 'Mad Dog' on account of his perceived aggressive approach to litigation – I would describe it as fearlessness – he and his family could not have been more generous, supportive and hospitable towards me and my own family. If one were to ask what Arnold Schwarzenegger, Sylvester Stallone and Bruce Willis have in common, the answer – as far as I am concerned – is that they have all been introduced to me by Marty as clients over the years. Marty is not only a respected and feared lawyer, but he has also developed incredible friendships with these and many, many more A-listers, famous musicians and sports personalities. He and his family have been the most good-natured and interesting hosts to us that anyone could ever wish for, and I can see why Marty generates such intense loyalty from his clients.

Over the years, my wife Selena and I have developed longstanding friendships with other LA-based attorneys. These friendships have not only provided great craic and excellent company, but have also opened my eyes to the Californian lifestyle and the opportunities out there that we can only dream about on my side of the Atlantic, and, of course, how the media attorneys operate in that jurisdiction.

FROM HOLYWOOD TO HOLLYWOOD

My wife – a successful lawyer in her own right – and I also had the benefit of renting an amazing house in Beverly Hills over a number of summers between 2012 and 2017 (not nearly as expensive as you might think, and certainly better value than comparable locations in Europe). This in turn, provided us with a very convenient staging post, not only to entertain clients but also as a springboard to getting a better understanding of how the other half lives.

I also had many interesting, one-off experiences. For instance, legendary attorney Neville Johnson brought me along to listen in to one of the private investigator Anthony Pellicano wiretapping trials, during which Pellicano represented himself, in his prison overalls, with Kirk Kerkorian, the billionaire businessman, in the witness box. This scandal gave rise to lengthy criminal proceedings involving not only Pellicano's alleged unlawful activity, but also dragging in many famous legal and other personalities. Only in America!

We also got to know Tony Glassman, who was a renowned sportsman in his day and who went on to become a very successful attorney. His clients were diverse, including the Church of Scientology and Hugh Hefner, with Hugh Hefner's annual pyjama party being an experience I will never forget. However, this was a much less exotic, and more corporate-style, event in its later years when Tony arranged for my wife and I to attend.

My US connections then began to take on legs of their own, with instructions coming in via meeting publicists and talent management agencies and, more significantly, one of the leading corporate 'fixers', Mike Sitrick. I also received referrals from the best-known criminal lawyer, Blair Berk, when it came to managing the media onslaughts raining down on some of her celebrity clients.

* * *

Having acted for politicians from across the divide on the Island of Ireland and in many other parts of the world, ironically I found most of them to share the very same problems, concerns and objectives. I am probably the only person to receive Christmas cards from both Gerry Adams and Ian Paisley.

I have also acted for former taoisigh. In my early days I had to stand back to understand the subtle complexities of Irish politics, but I think I got there in the end. However, I have often wondered why they cannot reach common political ground between each other on the fundamental issues of the day, when they come across as totally reasonable and genuine in discussing their own legal problems with me. I have also been consulted by many journalists, on both sides of the Irish Sea, some of whom had previously been at the receiving end of complaints I had initiated on behalf of other clients. Indeed, I have always had a soft spot for journalists and politicians, as both groups tend to be the target of gratuitous and malicious attacks merely because they are trying to do their respective jobs, and they are just as entitled to protect their reputations as wealthy businessmen.

I would express the same sentiments in relation to the different religions that have sought my assistance over the years. I have acted for and against the Catholic Church, provided opinions for ministers at either end of the spectrum of Protestantism, and for several decades I have provided advice to the Church of Scientology and its leader, David Miscavige. The latter have certainly kept me busy, in the context of incessant attacks from former, disaffected members of the Church. Perhaps significantly, the most often repeated allegations by those out to undermine David Miscavige has been the claim that his wife Shelly has gone missing and has been held as a prisoner somewhere within the Church organisation. This is despite that fact that the Los Angeles Police Department satisfied themselves that Shelly has, in accordance with her own wishes, been living a low-profile life and guarding her personal privacy.

Indeed, I also secured an IPSO (the UK equivalent of the Irish Press Ombudsman) adjudication in favour of David Miscavige and Tom Cruise regarding a totally inaccurate article on a 'bromance' between them.

I have aways found David Miscavige to be good company and very forthright in tackling any allegations head on. Unfortunately, in common with many newer religions, a number of those who have joined the Church for assistance or a crutch can often be disappointed if they do not receive a quick fix. Likewise, if they have been subjected to criticism from within, this can lead to resentment and perceived disillusionment. I can certainly envisage the difficulties in guiding and administering a large religious organisation, whether the Church of Scientology or the Catholic Church.

Perhaps I have the ultimate advantage in that I do not belong to any religious organisation or political party myself, which I like to think gives me the necessary independence to facilitate objective advice to my clients. I suppose learning to navigate and survive the risks and uncertainties of Northern Irish politics throughout the Troubles provided me with a very useful skill set when it came to acting for people from different religious and cultural backgrounds.

✻ ✻ ✻

In June 2006 the headline on the front page of the Belfast *News Letter* read, 'BRITNEY BRIEFS BELFAST LAWYER'. The reason I had been instructed by Britney Spears to put several publications on notice had been due to their publishing stories claiming that her marriage to Kevin Federline was over. When the stories initially appeared in *The National Enquirer*, it seemed as though there wasn't much that Britney could do about it. Up to that point, most US stars had to try to ignore what was written about them, hoping that the stories would soon lose traction. However, *The National Enquirer* had by then launched a European edition, which meant they had inadvertently submitted to European defamation and privacy laws. This, combined with Britney's international reputation and the extensive online coverage, meant that she could take legal proceedings against the publication under UK libel laws.

Indeed, while I was intending to take action, if necessary, in each of the UK and Irish jurisdictions, I had only got as far as putting the publisher on notice of our intention to proceed in the High Court in the UK or Ireland and a subsequent exchange of correspondence, when they and their lawyers, quite sensibly, decided that they would have serious problems in defending the case. To be fair to them, they did not force Britney into the inevitable stress of legal proceedings and agreed to settle the case, a settlement which included a formal apology.

I will never forget watching on my computer screen as this apology travelled from Ireland across Europe and the Far East to Australia and LA before I had time to draw breath. This was a pivotal moment for me professionally – it becoming apparent that it no longer mattered where we obtained an apology because the internet meant it could be propelled back through the online stratosphere with the same speed and prominence as the offending article.

Although Britney believed that her marriage was secure at the time I was consulted, the couple separated just a few months later. If nothing else, this sudden development was a stark illustration of time being of the absolute essence in libel litigation.

The three factors that had played a key part in the Britney Spears case – the existence of a European edition of the publication, the fact that she was someone with an international reputation and the global online dissemination

– formed the basis for the tsunami of claims that followed from Hollywood A-listers and other American household names, taking advantage of – as they were most certainly entitled to – the more claimant-friendly legal regimes on my side of the Atlantic.

Unsurprisingly, it is Hollywood A-listers and international personalities who attract the most intrusive media attention, for the obvious reason that their name or photograph sells tabloid newspapers and also generates enhanced interest, and often controversy, on social media platforms. For years, many US celebrities had become resigned to being tabloid fodder.

However, now there was an opportunity not only set the record straight but also to deter publication of false allegations in the future because vindication could be achieved in the form of an apology that could be pumped back across the internet in the same manner that the offending allegations had been published in the first place.

Britney Spears's case had been the first step that led to a list of world-famous personalities consulting me, including Jennifer Lopez, the Jenners/Kardashians, Justin Timberlake, Ashton Kutcher, Tony Robbins, Harrison Ford, Johnny Depp, Jennifer Aniston and many others. Even the reports in the media of these famous clients taking legal action provided them with a certain level of immediate international vindication because it demonstrated their outrage and determination to set the record straight. It also did no harm to my brand and the marketing of my work … at little or no additional financial expense.

If sometimes the subject allegations appeared trivial to some sections of the public, the consequences for the celebrity in terms of damage to their valuable brand, whether for future movie roles or merchandising deals, could potentially run into million-dollar losses. In some more extreme cases, there has been a threat to life from stalkers or those harbouring a grudge. The mental impact and trauma inflicted in these circumstances depends very much upon the state of mind of the person concerned at that particular time. Britney, for instance, was subjected to media scrutiny and criticism on an unprecedented level. Other clients have had suicidal thoughts, such have been their fears and distress over the consequences of people believing false allegations against them. I often liken myself to a dentist: nobody really wants to be consulting me unless they are in considerable pain. The bottom line is that these successful, and extremely busy, people would not be wasting time threatening litigation or seeking redress unless it was of the utmost importance to them. If anyone comes to me looking only for financial compensation, that is a warning flag – most of the big names who have consulted me over the years are only interested in getting the record set straight and achieving reputational vindication at the earliest possible opportunity.

In the past, many of the global publishers and plat-forms were based in the safe haven of the US, where it is very challenging, to say the least, to successfully sue for defamation due to the protections afforded by the First Amendment of the US Constitution and what is known as a 'public figure' defence. Most people who hold any public office, even at a relatively low level, are considered public figures, which means they have to establish actual malice on the part of the publisher of the defamatory material in order to have any prospect of success.

Even the wealthiest and most famous personalities have often found themselves unable to defend salacious allegations made against them in the USA. An historic example of this occurred in 1984, when Frank Sinatra attempted to sue Kitty Kelley for misrepresentation of facts in her unauthorised biography of his life. Apparently, Sinatra spent $2 million in legal fees attempting to stop publication. After abandoning the litigation, a spokesman for Sinatra stated that he 'had no wish to abridge (Ms) Kelley's First Amendment rights and that the public and critics were free to judge the book when it appears'. The publishers, Bantam Books, on Kelley's behalf, stated that 'not only did his case have no merit, it was also a violation of her First Amendment rights'. Kelley implied in the book that Sinatra was involved in criminality and was having an extra-marital affair with the former First Lady, Nancy Reagan, neither of whom ever sued successfully for defamation. The book became a bestseller following the coverage of the legal battle prior to publication: the 'Barbra Streisand' effect – of giving more publicity to an allegation than the original publication had – in full swing even before the term had been coined.

This case is an illustration of the protections afforded to the defendant rather than the plaintiff under the US

Constitution and explains why many Americans take the decision to head overseas to seek vindication for their reputations.

The obstacles facing potential litigants in the USA have been compounded by anti-SLAPP (Strategic Lawsuit Against Public Participation) motions. A SLAPP is defined as a lawsuit often taken by a wealthy person with the aim of suppressing stories that are of public interest. The SLAPP aims to intimidate or exhaust (financially and psychologically) the opponent. Most people would, of course, condemn this kind of litigation, but the problem is that anti-SLAPP motions seem to have had the effect in the USA, and in California in particular, of discouraging the ordinary person on the street from taking legal action to vindicate their reputation, given the risk of having the case struck out and costs awarded against the claimant in the early stages.

Nonetheless, the various hurdles imposed under US law contributed to what became a welcome cottage industry for me, when I was able to offer the alternative jurisdictions of the UK and Ireland to US clients who were frustrated by their inability to protect their good names in their home country.

Such was the publicity surrounding these early cases that President Obama, as a result of representations before various congressional committee hearings, was persuaded to introduce the grandly named Securing the Protection of our Enduring and Established Constitutional Heritage (SPEECH) Act in 2010. The purpose of the Act is to prevent

US citizens from suing US entities in foreign jurisdictions – it makes foreign libel judgments unenforceable in the US courts, unless the foreign legislation applied offers at least as much protection as the US First Amendment, or unless the defendant would have been found liable even if the case had been heard under US law. The Act created a basis for claiming damages against a foreign libel plaintiff, if they acted to deprive an American of their right to free speech. However, to the best of my knowledge, the provisions have rarely been implemented, and in my opinion the law has more of a political purpose and in the end can only serve to disadvantage US citizens.

To a large extent, this legislation came about as a result of campaigning by Dr Rachel Ehrenfeld, an American citizen who believed that she had been treated unfairly by the UK courts. In January 2004 Ehrenfeld had received an email from a London law firm acting on behalf of a Saudi billionaire, Khalid bin Mahfouz, threatening to sue her for libel for statements contained in her book *Funding Evil: How Terrorism is Financed and How to Stop It*.

Nine months after the initial contact between Ehrenfeld and the lawyers acting for the Saudi claimant, a libel action was filed in the High Court in London. Ehrenfeld's response was to decline to appear in court to defend the allegations asserted with considerable confidence in her book. As a result of her decision not to be represented at the hearing, Mr Justice Eady, the British judge presiding over the case, ruled against the author by default and ordered her to pay a total of £110,000, primarily for legal fees. The judge commented that, although under English law, Ehrenfeld had had the opportunity 'to prove, on the balance of probabilities, that the defamatory allegations were substantially true' and that 'the claimants have indicated that they are quite prepared to meet any such defence on its merits', 'no one has ever put forward such a defence, or any material which would be capable of substantiating a plea of justification'.

One of the reasons given by Rachel Ehrenfeld for her decision not to defend her allegations in the London High Court was the risk of incurring substantial legal fees. This argument possibly overlooks the fact that, under the UK legal system, costs are normally awarded to the successful party. This key difference between UK and US libel laws, of which her advisers would surely have made her aware, suggested that this aspect of Ehrenfeld's justification for not participating did not hold water. Another line of argument that Ehrenfeld put forward was that Mahfouz's decision to take action through the British courts was another example of 'libel tourism' – an exploitation of the more plaintiff-friendly UK libel laws as a means of achieving a vindication that the US system would not allow.

Ehrenfeld argued that Mahfouz was not sufficiently well-known in the UK to be able to claim potential damage to his reputation in that jurisdiction. The author also maintained that her book had been published in the US only and, as such, was intended exclusively for a US readership. The fact that twenty-three copies of the book had been obtained online in the UK was, she insisted, a mere glitch and did not constitute a substantial breach of libel laws. The Saudi businessman's lawyers countered by asserting that Mahfouz was bringing proceedings in the UK because he maintained residences and transacted business in this country and therefore *did* have a reputation to protect in the jurisdiction. As a result, Mr Justice Eady dismissed Ehrenfeld's accusations of 'forum shopping' as 'tendentious and a misrepresentation of the true position'. As for the writer's assertion that the book was intended for a US readership only, this was somewhat naive in an age when the internet has all but eliminated international borders, and where information is disseminated globally at the click of a mouse.

The campaign that followed has had a far-reaching impact in the US and elsewhere. However, although the SPEECH Act did put a brake on new clients coming to me from the US for a period, the impact was short-lived.

To read the national press, you would think that libel tourists had been descending on the UK and Ireland like triffids, crossing the Atlantic in their droves. However, despite my repeatedly asking for examples of so-called libel tourism, nobody – whether journalists or politicians in the Dáil, Westminster or the US Congress – has been able to cite even one instance that could be properly classified as such. Nonetheless, scaremongering has been frequently used to support the clamour for defamation law reform, perhaps in the absence of any other compelling reason. Some politicians have of course, particularly in the run-up to an election, been enthusiastic advocates for reform in order to pander to the media in the hope that it will bring some favourable press coverage for them at such a crucial time.

Two cases in particular, both of which I initiated on behalf of internationally renowned US personalities, have been cast up to me as examples of this rare beast. In September 2014, *Heat* European magazine had published an article implying difficulties in Justin Timberlake and Jessica Biel's marriage, and falsely attributing quotes to Jessica Biel. We achieved an early settlement in proceedings, which we had issued in the High Court in Dublin. The settlement included an apology to be announced before the court with a view to vindicating my clients and having the record set straight.

We had every right and reason to select Ireland as the appropriate jurisdiction – there had been just as many copies of the offending magazine displayed and sold per capita in Dublin as there had been in London, and our objective was to secure the earliest possible hearing date in order that the retraction of the false story could be disseminated online at the earliest opportunity. The defendant publishers had not argued strongly against this course of action and, given that the story was in the English-language edition sold in the UK and Ireland, there was no logical or legal reason for us not to avail of the convenience of the Dublin as opposed to the London courts. The only objections, of course, would come from the media at large, trying to create a perception of libel tourism, possibly on the basis that the High Court in

Dublin does not have the same stature as its counterpart in London.

The second example is the case I brought for the US motivational speaker, Tony Robbins, against BuzzFeed and Twitter. BuzzFeed initially moved to challenge jurisdiction, on the basis that the claim should have been brought in the US, where Robbins resides and BuzzFeed's main holding company is based. However, the court accepted our arguments that he had an international reputation, his books were sold by Irish retailers and his motivational talks attracted many Irish people. It was, in fact, BuzzFeed UK we were suing, along with Dublin-based Twitter International.

In a judgment stretching to eighty-five paragraphs, Mr Justice Mark Heslin gave an extremely detailed and comprehensive reasoning behind his conclusion that our client had satisfied the fundamental jurisdictional requirements, including his having a reputation and there being sufficient publication within the Irish jurisdiction. This clarified the position for any other international clients in similar circumstances.

I cannot, for client confidentiality reasons, go into the details of specific cases but I mention what is in the public domain to highlight the entitlement of globally known personalities to take legal action in each and every jurisdiction where they have suffered harm, and that the Irish courts are just as capable of determining these matters as any other judicial system.

The gap between defamation laws in the US and the UK was narrowed to some degree following the introduction of the Defamation Act in 2013, applicable to England and Wales, which requires claimants to establish that England is the 'proper' jurisdiction for a case to be brought when a defendant is not actually resident there. However, this legislation had been drafted primarily with the so-called libel tourists supposedly coming in from the US in mind, as opposed to wealthy Russian litigants taking advantage of still relatively claimant-friendly UK libel laws.

The claims that London is deluged with libel tourists has also been disproved by the statistics. Legal publishers Sweet & Maxwell, a subsidiary of publishing giant Thomson Reuters, found in research that the allegation of misuse of the UK legal system by libel tourists is without any real merit, when only three out of eighty-three defamation cases reported in the UK back in 2009–10 (when the study was conducted and the change in legislation was being debated) showed any hallmarks of 'libel tourism'.

Instagram, TikTok and Facebook have, of course, created a new wave of internationally recognisable internet entrepreneurs and brands. In the past, it was really only Hollywood A-listers and global business leaders who could argue that they were known and had a reputation in most of the countries in the world. However, in recent years, we have represented a number of successful influencers who have had their work undermined, their images misused, or somebody trying to undermine their promotion. The world is now a global village, and most celebrities have an international profile as a result of the internet – it's my firm belief that they should be facilitated in being entitled to protect their reputation in each and every country where they can prove it has been damaged, with the onus being on them to establish that damage.

FOUR

Taking on Amazon

In the earlier years of my career, all the letters I forwarded about defamatory content – almost without exception – had been directed to print and broadcast media. Most of these publishers had their own in-house legal departments, and I could engage directly with one of their lawyers to try to get the complaint resolved without recourse to litigation. This worked most of the time. Nowadays, dealing with Big Tech, it is not only almost impossible to engage with a human being, but it is equally a challenge to get any satisfaction out of one of their AI platforms. I have also encountered varying degrees of difficulty when seeking to persuade the online retailers to at least suspend distribution of an offending book until the courts have adjudicated on a libel complaint. It can take many months, if not years, to reach a hearing. This means that any judgment will be too late because so much damage will already have been done in the intervening period.

An early experience of defamatory content being disseminated internationally came when I was consulted by ten people – journalists and police officers – who had been the subject of the most serious and outrageous allegations in *The Committee: Political Assassination in Northern Ireland* by Sean McPhilemy. This book – one of the most controversial of its time – had been published in 1998 by Roberts Rinehart, a US publisher based in Boulder, Colorado. Although the print edition had initially only been distributed in the USA, there was significant publicity about it in the UK and Irish press, and it was widely available for sale via internet distributors such as Amazon.

The main contention of this book had been that each one of the people who would become my clients had been members of or in some way connected with an alleged secret 'committee' operating within Northern Ireland in the 1980s and 1990s, whose members had colluded for years with prominent loyalist paramilitaries to execute selected targets from the Catholic population. The full names of twenty-four members of this 'committee' – including that of the Nobel Prize-winning former Ulster Unionist leader, David Trimble – had been listed in an appendix at the back of the book.

Not only was this group of people facing serious reputational damage, but of even more concern had been that the allegations represented a potential threat to life. Many of these people had worked on the front line through the worst years of the Troubles, so most – if not all – of them had faced ongoing threats to their personal security. What made things different was that this was now the age of the internet, and their details were all over the worldwide web. This created great urgency in my work – I needed to stop distribution of the book and get a formal retraction and apology announced in a court of law.

From the outset, most of the distributors robustly denied any liability, leaving me with no alternative but to arrange for the issue of a total of seventy-two Writs of Summons, one of the largest number issued regarding one book in UK and Irish legal history. The BBC described it as 'the single biggest libel action in the UK'.

These legal actions were not just a major challenge before the judicial system on this side of the Atlantic – where there was limited if any experience of online dissemination – but were also a credit to the determination and resilience of the plaintiffs, respected journalists and police officers. The former group helped me with the extensive research that was needed. Unfortunately, it was well-nigh unthinkable to take legal action in the US, with the First Amendment and other protections offered to publishers and writers in that jurisdiction.

We met with serious resistance. Roberts Rinehart were utterly unrepentant and even defiant. Their attitude was self-assured and more than a little sanctimonious: they truly believed, they said, that they were serving the greater good by publishing the book in the interests of all Catholics in Northern Ireland as well as those in the US who considered themselves Irish-Americans. This sense of a personal crusade had evidently been adopted by one of their lawyers, whose responses to my correspondence were inflammatory to say the least. Rather than offering any prospect of a reasonable settlement or finding some form of common ground, he only made matters worse. Our relationship began to deteriorate even more when a copy of my initial letter of claim was forwarded to a well-known Irish republican website for publication online. I regarded this highly provocative action as, in some respects, an attempt to intimidate me.

However, my primary focus had always been the major online distributors of the book. Although the book was supposedly published and distributed exclusively in America, copies were available to purchase from major online booksellers from almost anywhere in the world, including of course in the UK and Ireland, the very jurisdictions where its publication and dissemination would cause the most damage to my clients.

Not only were the online distributors effectively offering the US edition of *The Committee* for sale internationally, but they were actively advertising the book in order to attract the widest possible readership. Sections of online commentary also featured an increasing number of posts or personal reviews, many of which were prejudiced and defamatory. They had not undergone any effective vetting process. One of these featured reader reviews actually called for the addresses of the alleged members of the 'committee' to be given to the IRA, so that they could be dealt with in what the reader deemed an appropriate way.

Anyone who posts their views online can be liable for any defamatory content, as is the distributor responsible for the website on which the offending posts appear and the Internet Service Provider (ISP). However, in practical terms, it is often difficult to pursue individual contributors. Often, they do not supply their real names, don't have to give an address, or they live outside the relevant jurisdiction. Even if it's possible to track them down, they often do not have any money with which to pay damages or the costs expended in going after them.

It is therefore more pragmatic to go after the distributors and/or the ISPs. The proviso is that distributors and ISPs can claim not to be aware of the content on their sites. This gives them a certain degree of legal protection, in that they must be afforded an opportunity to take down or address the offending allegations with the primary publisher. However, if they are put on notice and are made aware of the fact that they have published defamatory material and do not take appropriate remedial action within a reasonable period, they do – or should – become legally liable in many jurisdictions.

In terms of offering a book for sale that contains potentially defamatory content, booksellers and other retailers have recourse initially to what is called an 'innocent dissemination' defence, along with a degree of legislative protection on either side of the Atlantic. In their capacity as third-party distributors of an independently originated product, they cannot be held accountable for the content of every book they offer for sale. However, once they have received written notice that there may be a problem with the content of a specific book in their inventory, in my opinion they should be subject to the legal consequences of any failure to check out the problem and take appropriate action.

In the case of *The Committee*, the likelihood of the book containing potentially defamatory content should have been obvious to a distributor at first glance, given its damning subtitle and the publicity that heralded its publication.

In the event, the claims against Amazon and other internet book sellers were ultimately resolved on confidential terms, with the following statement read out by Amazon's counsel before the High Court in Belfast in December 2003:

> Amazon do not endorse the book's contents and have never sought to suggest there is any truth in the statements contained in the book.
>
> While it is accepted that Amazon cannot check each and every book distributed by them, and they are entitled to protect their fundamental right to freedom of expression and a right to free speech, Amazon wish to disassociate themselves from any defamatory content that may be contained in the book.

This litigation was groundbreaking in its day, and would have been very difficult to sustain if I had not had the full and unequivocal support and assistance of the clients. Although I knew they deserved to be vindicated, as we approached the door of the court, the result felt very much up in the air, bearing in mind the lack of any relevant precedent and the volume of the claims. I did get some degree of (bewildered) comfort, however, from Amazon's formal defence, which included a denial of liability based on First Amendment protection. Presumably somebody eventually told them that this fundamental basis of the US Constitution would not apply in Northern Ireland!

I have a certain amount of sympathy for the likes of Amazon and WH Smith, given the number of books they promote on a daily basis and the obvious difficulties in having each edition properly checked and legalled. Nonetheless, at the risk of repeating myself, once they are put on notice, and have a full and detailed case in front of them, then they should be obliged to suspend the book's availability temporarily while they undertake an appropriate investigation and legal assessment. I also believe that distributors should have a strict obligation to carefully consider any reviews or other commentary on a book published on their website, bearing in mind that these would not only be quick for them to read, but also provide an early indicator of controversial content within a book.

One thing is certain, given the stratospheric expansion of Amazon in recent years and their rise to world book-selling domination in general, we are going to witness many more legal battles on these and related issues.

To be fair to most of the online distributors, I have found them to be more responsive on occasion now than in the early days, and hopefully this co-operation will continue in at least proper consideration being given to any complaint from an early stage. Publishers are also much more cautious about having a book carefully legalled prior to going to print, thereby removing, or at least dramatically reducing, any risk of a subsequent complaint.

The contradictions and paradoxes attaching to the banner of free speech again come to the fore here. On the one hand, free speech in the US is often taken as a right to libel and to say anything, provided it is not spoken with malice. There are of course a number of exceptions, but litigating to vindicate a reputation in the US is certainly not for the faint-hearted. Different standards apply in European jurisdictions, but in both scenarios, there remains that very grey area of what constitutes free speech, or specifically justifies its protection.

Most people maintain that they are entirely in favour of free speech, but understandably this comes with a qualification that they don't agree with racist outbursts, for instance, or bullying comments. Of course, the problem remains as to who determines the issue and whether it is possible to delineate in clear and categoric terms what is or should be allowed. However, the bottom line has to be that 'free speech' ought to be 'fair and accurate speech', which most certainly was not the case so far as the content of *The Committee* was concerned.

FIVE

Can Fame and Privacy Ever Be Compatible?

My media practice began to expand rapidly as we entered the first decade of the twenty-first century. I was beginning to generate more work in the US, but most still came from the UK and Ireland, with not only the tabloid press finding themselves in the libel courts, but also the more conservative – and respected – media sometimes in the firing line as well.

While most of my work in those days was still for Irish and UK artistes, ranging from Van Morrison to The Corrs and Chris de Burgh, I was beginning to be contacted more by equally well-known claimants from the corporate, political and media worlds. Indeed, at this stage, journalists became the largest group of clients consulting me, followed closely by politicians and members of the legal profession. I saw the patronage of these groups as a kind of backhanded compliment, not least because many of them had, in the past, been on the receiving end of my professional correspondence, and I have become great friends with many journalists whose work I have always respected and admired. As well as the late Liam Clarke in his *Sunday Times* and *Belfast Telegraph* days, I was consulted by Jim McDowell and Hugh Jordan of the *Sunday World*, the former being one of many senior editors who at one stage or another was also a client as well as an adversary. This could not happen in the US where lawyers only act for *either* plaintiffs or defendants during their career.

All in all though, it was often the tabloid media that acted as though they had free rein to sensationalise and exaggerate their stories. And in this context, George Best once said of himself, 'I was the one who took football off the back pages and put it on to page one.' The tabloid interest in him continued throughout his life and even after his death in November 2005. Just a couple of days after he had died, his sister Barbara McNarry and her husband, Norman, got in touch with me. Stories that were often inaccurate and defamatory were appearing in publications including the *Daily Mail* and *Hello* magazine. Although you cannot libel the dead, the living relatives of the person who has died should at least be entitled to some degree of respect and consideration in a time of mourning. George's father, Dickie, received a list of questions from a tabloid on the eve of his son's funeral that were grossly intrusive, not to say highly insensitive. There followed a rollercoaster ride for the family, as no sooner had one report been corrected and an apology published than another story appeared.

All the while, Barbara – the residual beneficiary under George's will – was trying to get to grips with and administer George's legacy and the responsibilities that went with it. In fact, the estate was extremely modest, comprising limited equity in his London Cheyne Walk flat and the intellectual property right to his name and image. The only other bequest was a watch left to his son, Calum. By the time the mortgage on the property and George's debts had been settled, there was little equity left in the flat, and the IP rights were not the golden egg that people thought they were, or certainly what they would have been in the current era.

In some ways, George had much in common with David Beckham: both had worn the number 7 shirt for Manchester United; both received unprecedented levels of media coverage; both went to the lucrative US soccer league towards the end of their careers. However, George came from a different era – before the vast incomes enjoyed today by star players and the lucrative sponsorship and advertising deals. Another key difference was that George was an alcoholic, and his battles with the booze probably received more coverage over the years than his dazzling performances on the pitch. With competition from so many living celebrities, George's legacy was always going to be extremely difficult to monetise.

However, I never found Barbara to be motivated by financial gain for herself. She had genuine altruistic objectives, which led to her setting up the George Best Foundation, a charity founded with the aim of enabling young people to advance their football skills. I was asked to join the inaugural board, which I agreed to do for a limited period of time, given my extensive work commitments. The charity was a great credit to the McNarrys, though it was eventually wound up primarily due to the administrative challenges faced by such a high-profile charity. It had imposed immense time demands on and caused considerable stress to Norman and Barbara.

Around this time, there had been increasing public interest in the work of libel lawyers, not least due to their acting for celebrities. In 2010, I received an approach from a well-known producer, Ross Wilson, who was preparing a series of programmes for the BBC based on the work of media lawyers. Ross made a choice about which cases he felt it would be most appropriate to feature, with the relevant clients' consent, of course. In the first, I was acting for the Israeli mentalist and performer Uri Geller – best known for his spoon-bending prowess – against the US TV network CNN. I had already brought a number of earlier claims for Uri to a successful conclusion, all of which involved his friendship with Michael Jackson. At the time Uri consulted me, there was still considerable controversy over the interview Jackson gave to Martin Bashir, which was broadcast as the documentary *Living with Michael Jackson* in February 2003 and had led to Jackson's arrest on criminal charges. There was speculation in the media that Uri had profited from facilitating the interview – in fact, Uri had given any money he had received directly to charity. However, the celebrity status of both men fed into media speculation, not to mention the fact that Michael Jackson had been best man when Uri and his wife had renewed their vows in 2001.

Of course, these circumstances provided the perfect background for one of the episodes of the BBC's *See You in Court* series, particularly with Uri being the ultimate performer and a master at communication. Much of the footage was filmed at Uri's wonderful property in Sonning in Berkshire, not far from London and on the banks of the River Thames. Uri was able to add colour to the episode with a car covered in bent spoons in the background and anecdotes about his association with many famous people. There was never a dull moment with Uri. On one occasion when I called to visit him, I was introduced to the late Kenneth Kaunda, the former president of Zambia, who had been sleeping on the couch in Uri's sitting room.

The next episode involved the Galway-based ultra-marathon runner, Richard Donovan, who organised an annual North Pole marathon. This event featured in an article in *Forbes* magazine, which implied that he had taken risks in relation to the safety of the participants. These false allegations included a claim that luggage had been stacked at the emergency exit of the plane in which the participants travelled and that a bulldozer was in a dangerous position close to the landing strip. The clear inference was that Richard had recklessly endangered the lives of his charges. Not only were these defamatory allegations unfounded, but Donovan had irrefutable evidence to rebuff the claims

– *Forbes* didn't realise that the inside of the plane had been videoed by another reporter, and the footage showed that the safety doors were not blocked by luggage and that the landing conditions were not unsafe.

This litigation turned out to be a marathon in its own right in that my initial overtures to *Forbes*'s legal department were rebuffed. Unfortunately, I made the mistake of attempting to take them on within their own New York jurisdiction. I ultimately had to advise the client to withdraw due to the escalating cost risks and the onerous hurdles faced under NY law. Instead, with the production team filming all the time, I transferred the battle to London, Dublin and Belfast.

Although *Forbes* appeared to be continuing to put up a robust defence, when we began to drive towards the door of the court in Belfast, their attitude suddenly changed, and we were able to resolve the matter on very satisfactory settlement terms, while producing some interesting viewing for the BBC production. I don't know whether the documentary brought me extra work – but it's worth remembering that lawyers have heavy restrictions placed on advertising, and so I was pleased to accept indirect marketing opportunities that came my way. I invited the Belfast-based lawyer acting for *Forbes* to participate, which he willingly did of his own volition, only to withdraw when his client demanded that he must do so shortly before the transmission date. This lawyer added to his own predicament by copying his client's inhouse lawyer in to an email. Although I did everything

I could to assist, the proverbial shit had hit the fan for him. I was at least able to persuade the documentary producer to delete the footage of his contribution.

My media law practice had grown rapidly in Ireland, even before the Big Tech companies moved there for tax reasons, and I had an intense run of cases on behalf of celebrities. One was Rosanna Davison, an Irish model and a former Miss World, who is the daughter of the singer and songwriter Chris de Burgh, also a client at the time. In 2009, Ryanair's charity calendar hadn't featured any Irish women, and a journalist asked Rosanna's opinion about this. She had replied, 'If I was [organising] it, I would have made sure that Irish women were involved because it's an Irish charity and Irish fundraising.' Her comment prompted Ryanair to issue a press release that said, 'Ryanair today hit back at comments made by Irish glamour model Rosanna Davison in relation to the absence of Irish cabin crew from Ryanair's 2009 charity calendar, which bordered on racism and demonstrated an elitist attitude against Ryanair's international cabin crew.' This release was defamatory, making Rosanna out to be racist, xenophobic and jealous.

Rosanna bravely took on Ryanair, who were determined to stick to their guns, thereby making legal proceedings inevitable. The case trundled on towards a full-blown hearing at the High Court in Dublin, which began in May 2011. I had anticipated from the beginning that some form of settlement proposal would be put on the table, but this never happened.

Although I always believed Rosanna had a solid case, I watched the twelve-person jury being empanelled with considerable trepidation as I tried to work out how they might react to a young model from a wealthy background with a famous father. There was no way that I could tell whether any had fallen foul of Ryanair's charging policies … or whether they were fans of Chris de Burgh.

The hearing began with Ryanair taking the same pugilistic approach they had adopted from the outset, which even included an attack on me personally for writing 'aggressive' letters. However, Judge de Valera kept very tight control on the proceedings from day one. Nonetheless, it was still very difficult to read the minds of the jurors, although there is normally some indication as a hearing progresses. As the case went on, it began to seem that at least two jury members were hostile to my client, judging by their facial expressions and demeanour when Rosanna was giving her evidence. One ended up standing down, and it became apparent that there was unlikely to be unanimous agreement between the jurors.

Rosanna showed remarkable stoicism and courage throughout the process, especially during the long wait for the jury's verdict. They eventually came back with a finding in Rosanna's favour and an award of €80,000. I was relieved and satisfied on the one hand; on the other, I felt disappointed that the damages were not the six-figure sum that I had anticipated: Rosanna had been dragged through the courts and the case brought additional pressure and much wider dissemination of the story.

Ryanair remained unrepentant and were dismissive about the award – but decided not to appeal. For my part, I received what I saw as a welcome compliment a short time later, when Ryanair approached me, offering me an annual retainer to act for them in media-related matters. I have acted for them and for their charismatic CEO Michael O'Leary ever since, and I must say that I have seen a completely different side to the company and to Michael, not least due to his hilarious sense of humour and astute judgement, and for whom I have the utmost admiration. He is a rare talent and a larger-than-life character; someone whose achievements are now legendary. I also got on very well with the Ryanair lawyers.

Louis Walsh, the X *Factor* judge and music impresario, first got in touch with me in 2011 following the most appalling libel against him that was published on the front page of *The Sun* and attributed to the newspaper's then entertainment editor. The allegation published in *The Sun* – that Louis had sexually assaulted someone in a nightclub toilet – was as outrageous as it was fabricated. Despite having this pointed out to them, the newspaper failed to act, and the allegations went viral – even though this was before social media had taken the extensive hold on society that it has nowadays.

I could not help but feel absolute sympathy for Louis from the outset. He came across as a very genuine, open and sensitive person – perhaps not always how he came over when he was on *X Factor*. The more I engaged with him, the more determined I was to get a result for him.

The story caused Louis enormous personal distress. The publishers of *The Sun* refused to back down. Even with us doing everything that we could to expedite, the legal process is slow, and getting a court hearing takes many months, if not years. We do try to generate early publicity around the fact that libel proceedings have been issued on behalf of the client to show that they are coming out fighting, expressing their outrage and robust denials. In the meantime, the victim of the libel – in this case Louis – has to live every hour and every day with the stigma and stress of the allegation hanging over them, not knowing if or when they will ever receive sufficient vindication to let them get their life back on track. This is why defamation damages tend to be much higher proportionately than personal injury awards. It is difficult to understand and assess, never mind put a figure on, the serious psychological impact of an attack on a person's integrity. The stain and stigma are likely to linger on regardless of any eventual legal outcome.

Louis put a brave face on things, and we did everything within our power to get the case into court quickly. The publishers of *The Sun* were eventually convinced by their legal advisors that they should settle, and settle they did for what is still an enormous sum – €500,000 – accompanied by a comprehensive retraction and apology. With all his years of experience in getting publicity for his musical protégées, Louis was at least able to ensure that this comprehensive vindication made as many headlines, if not more, than the original story.

One of the problems for many of my clients is that the law cannot keep up with the speed of today's media. In Louis' case, the completely false story about him was published in June 2011, but he did not receive the settlement and apology until November 2012. Although the problems brought to me by clients, no matter how famous they are, vary enormously, they all share one key feature: I need to work as quickly as possible.

Outside court, I made a statement, with Louis beside me. 'We are not trying to gag the press or stop investigations, but if there was a strong body that we could have rung before to get them to stop the story for twenty-four hours, we could have provided proof that Louis wasn't even in the place at the time and all this would have been avoided. They gave us just a few hours; they were determined to run it.' Louis himself described what had happened to him as something he wouldn't wish on his very worst enemy.

As I said that day, I feel strongly that publishers should give the subjects of their stories more time to respond. Louis had not even been in the club at the time of the alleged incident, and if there had been any desire to be fair and honest on the part of the tabloid, a few simple fact checks would have been all that was required. However, as has so often been the case over the years, the red tops were reluctant to let the truth stand in the way of a good story, which of course sold newspapers. Louis' misfortune was a classic example, with the consequences for the victim or the conscience of the journalist not on the agenda. Celebrity gossip and tittle tattle is one thing, but a malicious allegation of this nature is another matter altogether. It is a tribute to Louis' fortitude that he did not crack under the strain of having this hanging over his head for many, many months. I have always appreciated the trust he placed in me during this most difficult period of his life.

As one case leads to another, so too do multiple new instructions emanate from clients for whom we have won cases. Louis has built up unrivalled connections over the years; these contacts have also sometimes needed my help in their dealings with the media.

One of Louis' friends who consulted me was Tulisa Contostavlos, also an *X Factor* judge. In 2013 she had been the subject of a sting at the hands of the notorious Fake Sheikh, Mazher Mahmood, which led to her facing criminal proceedings. The allegation against her was that she had arranged for someone she knew to supply cocaine to Mahmood, who was posing as a film producer. The proceedings against Tulisa were eventually abandoned and Mahmood himself received a prison sentence for tampering with evidence during Tulisa's trial.

By the time the criminal proceedings ended, the period in which Tulisa could bring a defamation action had expired. In 2015 I was brought in to try to persuade the High Court in Ireland to grant a discretionary one-year extension so that we could bring a claim in that jurisdiction. Although this application was not successful, we had other strings to our legal bow and managed to get the matter resolved in Tulisa's favour.

Tulisa's case – although we were able to get it satisfactorily resolved – illustrates the importance of timing in defamation cases. Not only is there a strict twelve-month period from the date of publication within which to issue legal proceedings, but the speed with which a complaint is brought – and we are talking in terms of weeks here – can often have a major bearing on the credibility of a claimant and the assessment of the seriousness of the impact of the subject allegations. The President of the High Court in Ireland made it very clear that protective proceedings should have been issued in the UK within the statutory time limit, with the intervening criminal proceedings not being regarded as an acceptable reason for delay.

A year sounds like more than enough time to bring a case, but in some of the more serious cases, the trauma and ongoing fallout, not to mention the financial challenges and the prospect of funding of what can be extremely expensive litigation, can cause delay. The months pass by very quickly in the exchange of communications passing between the parties, while evidence gathering can also take up a significant amount of time. Furthermore, Tulisa's legal team will have been concentrating on defending the criminal proceedings as their immediate priority.

Tulisa was one of very many people affected by the actions of the Fake Sheikh. Another victim of one of his stings was Sarah Ferguson, the Duchess of York. In 2016 I was approached by a mutual friend, who asked if I would be prepared to advise Sarah. Some six years earlier, she had been misled and manipulated into giving the impression that she was offering access to her former husband, Prince Andrew, in return for a cash payment.

The financial and emotional pressure of taking legal action is huge, particularly for someone like the Duchess of York, who has been in the media spotlight for most of her adult life, with very little support and protection available to her. To take on the publishers of the *News of the World*, we had to think outside the box in terms of strategy and what we could achieve. We focused our complaint on the torts of conspiracy, malicious falsehood and deceit. While the basis of the first two may be obvious, the tort of deceit is not utilised as much in the English courts and is defined as 'a tort arising from a false statement of fact made by one person, knowingly or recklessly, with the intent that it shall be acted upon by another, who suffers damages as a result'.

A key factor was that the time limit for bringing a claim is six years, rather than the one year allowed for defamation proceedings to be issued. The financial risk is no less significant, however, but we were satisfied that Sarah had a good case. All credit to Sarah, for whom I have considerable admiration, she had the courage to give us the go-ahead to take on the mighty News Corporation, whose subsidiary company published the *News of the World*.

The terms negotiated when this action was eventually resolved have to remain strictly confidential, but both Sarah and I were very satisfied with the outcome.

Sarah may have been the author of some of her own controversies back in the day, but I could not help but get the feeling that she was often thrown under a bus to distract from the travails of other Royals. I have frequently told her that she must have been the subject of more vitriolic headlines and brutal press coverage than any other woman in the world. Although I have managed to secure a number of settlements and apologies for her, it has been impossible to deal with most of the defamatory articles and breaches of her privacy, such has been the antagonism towards her on the part of some journalists. Some of the more egregious examples have ranged from publication in one national newspaper of a photograph that had been taken by some charming person of the Duchess falling asleep while travelling on the London Tube. This was in contrast to the usual tabloid 'scoop' claiming that she had been guilty of extravagance and overspending when it's usually the case that she has been in receipt of a friend's largesse.

The Duchess has in my experience always been very stoical, although also understandably upset, about the ongoing attempts to undermine and embarrass her. However, not only is such reporting grossly unfair, but it also detracts from the extensive voluntary work she regularly undertakes for international and UK charities and good causes, many helping vulnerable and underprivileged children. In 1993 she founded Children in Crisis to provide education to forgotten children around the world, and the charity has educated over 1.4 million children. She was also a founder patron of Street Child, recently stepping down from this role to focus on her own recently launched international non-profit, Sarah's Trust. In its first project, at the start of the pandemic, the Duchess mobilised an ongoing national response to benefit over 150,000 NHS staff from care homes, hospices and emergency services.

It is a great pity that those begrudgers who do not hesitate to take a cheap shot at Sarah, are not prepared to give her some credit for all this good work. Knowing the dedication and priority that she has given to these charities, I find it frustrating that she receives very little media coverage, never mind acknowledgement, for this work – although I should add that credit is something that she has never sought.

The similarities between the Duchess and her late friend Princess Diana are striking: they both had difficult upbringings; they were both thrown at a young age into the global spotlight; they both tried to please others, often at the expense of their own interests; and their respective marriages ended in divorce. However, Sarah's matrimonial settlement was extremely modest in comparison to Diana's. She was left with no option but to go out into an unfamiliar corporate world, unprepared and fairly naïve, to try to look after herself. How Sarah has had the mental strength and stoicism to survive all the very public and often misogynistic attacks on her character, appearance and actions never ceases to amaze me.

While Sarah may have shown a lack of judgement in some of her associations, the problem is that she was not properly equipped or experienced to deal with some of the people who sought her patronage. Although there have been many people seeking to act in her best interests, there are others who have had less honourable motives and for whom she has been easy prey, having received little or no protection after stepping outside the family fold. Sarah has had to fight for herself her whole life. Unfortunately, in the modern, social media world, there is little room for error of judgement, particularly for those living a high-profile existence.

All of these cases have often prompted me to reflect on the price of fame. Sinéad O'Connor also suffered deeply at the hands of the press. In spite of her fame and talent, and the great courage she showed in speaking out about controversial issues that many others chose to ignore, her final years brought a significant amount of further distress and trauma for her. When she came to me around 2020, asking for assistance in relation to ongoing litigation against her, she had already spent a six-figure sum on representation, and she was terrified that she was about to lose her only tangible and solid asset – her family home. Of course, she also had her remarkable back catalogue, but the actual value of this was less certain, as was the question of whether it would offer immediate financial recourse for her. Although her legal woes were more contractual than media-related in nature – the latter being my normal area of practice at the time – I had enough relevant experience from my past professional life to be able to grasp the core legal issues immediately and move quickly and effectively in her best interests.

During our meetings and discussions, I was bowled over by her sanguine and philosophical attitude. She displayed no animosity during the course of my conversations with her. She came across to me as a determined but vulnerable person, whom I admired, even though I didn't necessarily share some of her opinions. When her death was announced in July 2023, I watched and listened to the many tributes and wondered what Sinéad would have made of it all. I did feel that it was a great pity that she did not receive a similar level of accolade and recognition during crucial periods of her often troubled life.

As the old adage goes, 'fame does not necessarily bring happiness', and what I've seen of many others in my own working life has proved this time and time again. In fact, the perception that those who have wealth and a glamorous profile automatically enjoy an idyllic lifestyle could not be further from the truth. In my experience, life for many of these people is made extremely difficult by begrudgers waiting in the wings to pounce almost gleefully on any misfortunes that may befall them.

* * *

It's also difficult to protect your privacy when you have a high profile in the media. Many of the problems that celebrities bring to me relate to breaches of their privacy or that of their family.

For a period, between 2016 and 2020, I engaged on a regular basis with the tabloids about the publication of paparazzi photographs of celebrities carrying or walking with their children in public. Ashton Kutcher and Mila Kunis had led the way in taking on the publisher Associated Newspapers; they were soon followed by many other clients ranging from the *Succession* star Kieran Culkin to *Die Hard* actor Bruce Willis filing complaints relating to similar types of publications. The tabloids often seemed to regard any famous celebrity as fair game – perhaps it's unrealistic to star in a box-office blockbuster and have an expectation of privacy if you are in public places; however, the members of a celebrity's family, particularly their children, are entitled to privacy, especially away from celebrity events. I always advise these clients to make sure that they don't ever put their child in the limelight or take them to red carpet events with photographers as this can be interpreted as the parent consenting to their child appearing in the press.

While most responsible publishers respected the privacy of the family, more aggressive tabloids printed the photographs that were taken on a daily basis by paparazzi who staked out children's playparks and the streets of Beverly Hills. Although this provided yet another cottage industry for us media lawyers, it was deeply frustrating and worrying for celebrity parents. Once the photograph had been published, a belated offer to blank out the face of a child was far too little too late. The concerns of these famous parents were raised further with real-life kidnappings, such as the Madeline McCann case, frequently making the news.

The problem, of course, became magnified in the era of social media when images circulate worldwide in a heartbeat, and also because of the advanced cameras and drones that are now widely available.

One particularly outrageous example involved the publication of aerial photographs of a very famous singer's private home, with notes on the photographs to show where he kept his vintage cars and his art collection – a burglar's dream. Again, although the photograph was taken down, the damage had already been done as soon as the tabloid hit the newsstands and the internet on the day of publication.

I have worked on many other serious invasions of privacy, which have had devastating impacts on the celebrity involved, especially when their children are the subject of the story, whether because of a serious medical condition or because they were going off the rails. Back in the day we were able to move for what is known as a 'super-injunction' prior to publication. The very existence of such an injunction could not be reported in order to protect the anonymity of the subject. I only ever used this process when there was a threat to life or the interests of children were involved. It has sometimes been the case that a client is facing such trauma as a result of a potential story that expert medical opinion has shown there to be a genuine risk of suicide. In my experience, judges were always very cautious in granting what I always regarded as a remedy of last resort.

I once applied for an injunction for a Hollywood A-lister in order to prevent the publication of medical information about his very young child. In the end, out of frustration at the ongoing, persistent media enquiries he was facing, he took the decision to make his child's diagnosis public rather than waiting until the child was older.

Nowadays, it is very rare for any party to apply for an injunction in relation to a defamation claim, super or otherwise, and even to ensure the protection of privacy. The problem is that it is almost impossible to secure any degree of privacy for any length of time in this era of social media, and an injunction does no more than extend that time for a limited period.

Even when the court strives to preserve the anonymity of a person in accordance with an order or other legislative safeguards, it is impossible to stop the worst kind of keyboard warriors from releasing the details via anonymous blog sites. The worst example of this is when victims of sexual crimes are named online. Victims of these kinds of crimes are entitled to lifelong anonymity, and their names are never reported in mainstream media unless they have waived their right to anonymity. However, their identities are often published online, and it is almost impossible at that point to take effective legal action. The plight of a victim in this kind of criminal trial is compounded by the fact that she (most victims are female) is classified as a witness and so isn't entitled to her own independent legal representation during what is often a vitriolic time in the witness box. Indeed, in one recent high-profile case the injured party had to face no less than four sets of lawyers, briefed by four separate defendants, as was their entitlement.

SIX

Watching My Back

Building a successful media law practice has brought with it a level of press interest and an increased media profile benefiting my clients, and, indirectly, myself and my firm, in terms of publicity. However, a number of my journalist clients have told me that several newspapers, including a leading Irish Sunday paper, had discouraged my name from appearing in print during the past twenty years with a view to depriving me of 'the oxygen of publicity'. Although this has been slightly frustrating, I suppose I cannot really blame them. As the late Liam Clarke – a great friend, client and former *Belfast Telegraph* political and *Sunday Times* (NI) editor – once said to me, 'newspapers do not have to be balanced, nor do they have to justify a position they have taken at any given time or on any particular subject'. In my younger days, I had thought that free speech and an unfettered press meant that there would be even and balanced reporting, and that media outlets would take a liberal and open – if not necessarily impartial – stance. In other words, the same approach I have taken in my career – I will act for anyone with a genuine case that has appropriate merit, regardless of their political, religious or other standing.

I still sometimes do get irritated, and somewhat concerned, by personal attacks that suggest that I am favouring one particular political or religious view, and doing so at the expense of my professional integrity. We media lawyers are often not only associated with our clients, but also sometimes criticised for having the temerity to provide them with legal representation on account of their conduct, reputation or the public perception of them. While my response has always been that I am first and foremost an officer of the court, and everyone should be entitled to the service of a lawyer, some of the tabloids and social media commentators just cannot help themselves. For example, when I came on record for an Israeli security consultant, one of his critics in the US immediately tweeted a critical reference to me having also acted for Prince Andrew. When acting for a former Northern Irish first minister, Peter Robinson, I was criticised for also having represented the former Sinn Féin president, Gerry Adams. In other words, some people cannot accept the independence of the legal profession and our calling to act for clients, whatever their political or religious persuasions, without fear or favour.

I have steadfastly remained politically neutral over the years, while respecting two leading counsel, and friends of mine whom I have always admired whom I have always admired professionally in their deciding to follow a parallel career at opposite ends of the political spectrum, and each in a different era, namely Bob McCartney (Unionist) and Jim O'Callaghan (Fianna Fáil). Nevertheless, both managed to resolutely maintain their independence and impartiality as lawyers.

Many years ago, I secured a damages settlement for Ian Paisley Jr from the *Daily Mail* as a result of an article written by the political commentator Ruth Dudley Edwards.

Ever since then, Dudley Edwards has publicly expressed her resentment towards me. This animosity comes to the fore in her annual end-of-year column for a local newspaper, in which she lists the people she would like to banish to a desert island. Of course, Ian Paisley and I are usually included near the top of the list. In 2021 she described me as 'solicitor Paul Tweed, whose unrelenting and successful opposition to reform of libel law has been a boon to politicians'.

I have always gone out of my way to try to negotiate settlements before litigation costs mount up. Apart from the fact that I have always had the good fortune to be inundated with work, and it is important for balancing my workload that at least a significant number of my cases settle early, it always makes absolute sense for most, if not all, of my clients to have their reputations vindicated at the earliest possible opportunity. This should also be a priority for a defendant publisher in terms of saving legal costs, but, for reasons known only to themselves, they are often reluctant to settle. One example springs to mind – a defamation claim my firm brought against the publishers of a local newspaper on behalf of a senior civil servant. Although I had made numerous attempts to settle early with their English-based lawyer, my efforts were scorned. Even the round-table mediation that I had encouraged turned into a farce, with a number of the representatives for the publisher playing a game of eyeballing me and adopting a hostile stance to try to intimidate me and my client. While I found this perplexing, if not downright absurd, at the time, I did have the advantage of having played a similar staring game on many occasions with my children when they were young. Unfortunately for the publishers' shareholders, this approach turned out to be a provocative and very costly mistake when they belatedly had to settle the case on substantial financial terms to the benefit of my client.

The most vindictive action directed at me came from within the BBC. It began with a request from them to the Law Society of Northern Ireland to consider whether Joe Rice – a leading criminal lawyer – and I had been in breach of the Society's regulations. Initially, they did not make a formal complaint or follow what would be regarded as the normal procedure for doing so. The BBC's enquiry, or submission, or whatever they were calling it, related to correspondence that the BBC claimed should have been furnished to them subsequent to the filing of affidavits in support of a High Court action (not defamation on this occasion). We had brought these proceedings on behalf of local businessman Frank Cushnahan, who had been the subject of two BBC *Spotlight* documentaries. The facts and merits of the case are, to a large extent, irrelevant to this issue, in that the BBC's detailed submission to the Law Society related to a purported objection regarding disclosure of certain correspondence subsequent to the filing of an affidavit.

I had never had a Law Society complaint made against me in over forty years of practice, and the BBC had carefully sidestepped describing their submission to the Law Society as such, at least in the first instance. What took both Joe and me aback was that this came completely out of the blue, many months after the appeal in the case had been resolved by mutual agreement in June 2017. The trial judge had gone out of his way to compliment us and the BBC's NI lawyers on our conduct during the legal proceedings, the hearing having run for a number of days. There had not been one iota of complaint from the BBC's legal team before, during or immediately following the hearing. Perhaps significantly, their Belfast lawyers, who conducted the defence of the proceedings on the BBC's behalf, were not party to this subsequent, and vexatious, action.

Not only had the BBC waited more than six months after the case had been (we had thought amicably) resolved before bringing up their concerns, but it then took the Law Society several months to even draw the BBC's 'letter of concern' to our attention – it had landed on the desk of the Society's Chief Executive just before Christmas 2017 (presumably with the objective of ruining my holiday period). In the meantime, I had been continuing to deal with the BBC's legal department, unaware of this developing scenario in the absence of any direct complaint to us. When I did finally learn of the letter, I provided an extremely detailed explanation and clarification to the Law Society regarding the issue raised, while expressing my own and Joe Rice's bewilderment that the BBC had taken this outrageous step. We demanded that the BBC be compelled to state whether or not this was an actual 'complaint'.

Significantly, in their failure to put their complaint to us in writing in the first instance, or having given us any prior notice of their intentions, they had deprived us of an opportunity to defend our position, as would have been the normal expectation for a 'complaint'. Of equal concern was the apparent failure of an unidentified BBC employee who prepared the letter to include what I regarded as all the relevant correspondence, in what was an otherwise voluminous bundle of documentation forwarded to the Law Society in support of their submission. Despite having complained bitterly about this apparent omission, no acceptable explanation had been forthcoming from them, I was therefore left to draw my own conclusion. In any event, our correspondence had in fact been placed before the court prior to and during the hearing, with no issues being raised by anyone at the relevant time.

The BBC did not provide us with the names of the main protagonists, while this apparent attempt to exact some form of belated revenge at the licence payers' expense was of considerable concern.

Although both Joe and I were totally vindicated by the Law Society, the BBC – on realising that they had failed to achieve their objective – promptly decided to change their approach and describe their submission as a complaint, in order to attract the protection of what is known as 'absolute privilege'. This is the same protection that attaches to parliamentary debate, and prevented Joe and I from suing them for defamation. We are both lawyers with considerable experience and long careers behind us, and knew from the outset that this enquiry-cum-complaint had no merit whatsoever. However, the whole experience would be a daunting challenge for anyone without similar professional knowledge and background.

I am sure that most lawyers have had experience of someone trying to undermine them.

On 1 March 2022 an MP, Bob Seely, used parliamentary privilege to name four well-known media lawyers and said about them:

> We have to wonder about the reputations that these people will end up with in a few years' time, even if they are behaving as well as they might – I am being careful in what I say. Perhaps they are really lovely people, but perhaps their amorality will really begin to bite their reputations in a way that will be uncomfortable.

Seely criticised the lawyers for acting for Russian clients regardless of the independent services they provided as officers of the court and the law that they are entitled to rely on at any given time.

Lawyers are always easy targets for criticism, and in this case the professionals concerned never sought to hide their identities or their work, but they were still exposed to a frenzy of rebuke from a number of quarters. As lawyer and writer David Allen Green pointed out in an astute article for *The Sunday Times*, the times have changed suddenly and dramatically from when the then Justice Minister, Lord McNally, had encouraged Russians to come to London to utilise the courts for their commercial disputes. His stance was vigorously and actively endorsed by the then Mayor of London – none other than Boris Johnson.

What is of concern is the tendency to associate a lawyer with their client; to tar them with the same brush. Examples have included an attempt to question the professional integrity of the Labour party leader, Sir Keir Starmer, as a result of his representing a terrorist, Abu Qatada, back in 2008. Dragging this to public attention again many years later is suggestive of some form of improper conduct on his part when he was doing nothing more than discharging his professional duties as an officer of the court. In a democracy, everyone is supposed to be entitled to independent legal representation.

In April 2022 US Congressman Steve Cohen, a lawyer himself, took matters to a new level when he said that a number of the UK's leading media lawyers should be denied entry to the US because they had represented

Russian oligarchs in the past, an outburst that appeared to me to have echoes of McCarthyism.

The Congressman is a respected campaigner for a number of causes, but I was nevertheless most disappointed by his stance on this occasion, as I was back in 2010, when he chaired a House Committee enquiring into so-called 'libel tourism'. I wrote to him at the time, asking if I could give evidence to his committee and also inviting him to provide even one solitary example of libel tourism on the part of US citizens in the jurisdiction of the UK. He failed to acknowledge my letter and appeared to be unable to cite any such cases when the issue was raised during his hearings.

The fundamental issue should always be whether the facts are correct and if everyone has been given a fair chance to argue their case prior to publication. Just as every member of the public, regardless of their financial resources, should be afforded access to the courts, wealthy and powerful people should not be allowed to bully or take advantage using their superior financial firepower. There must be a balance, always keeping the facts at the forefront.

Although I do understand concerns being expressed and action being taken against some of the Russian oligarchs, it is not the case that every wealthy Russian is corrupt or a supporter of President Putin. I understand that a colleague in the legal profession was reported to the Regulator by a government department primarily due to him seeking a legal remedy for a Russian client who had been sanctioned. Although this came to nothing, the very fact that we, as officers of the court, can be challenged and undermined, if not bullied, in this manner is a disturbing trend. Where does such interference in the performance of our professional duties end? Can government and regulatory bodies determine who is and who is not entitled to representation, and have actions such as these any place in a democratic society? The bottom line is that everyone should be entitled to legal representation, and to have the protection of the law of the land at any given time.

Over the years I have always taken pride and satisfaction in the fact that I have been able to act not only for claimants from all political and religious persuasions, but also for both print and online publishers, regardless of their size or stature. I believe that this has given me an added advantage in understanding how each side thinks and their concerns, and has also given me a certain degree of empathy for the particular stance my client may have adopted.

Unfortunately, it goes with the territory that the lawyers will often be in the firing line when open season is declared on a particular target. I have always taken the view that if I decide there is merit in a case, I will fight tooth and nail for that client, while advising them bluntly and robustly on the risks involved. If they fail to take my advice, then I sometimes have to step back from representing them. Occasionally, I have discovered that the client has not been entirely honest or has omitted a crucial detail. Then I have to decide whether or not I can continue to act for them. At the risk of repeating myself again, if they have a proper and appropriate case, they are entitled to legal representation, and, as an officer of the court, I should neither prejudge them nor decide not to act on the basis of any controversial circumstances in their background.

SEVEN

The Court of Public Opinion

Before I write anything about Prince Andrew, I should make clear that I utterly condemn the abhorrent conduct of the convicted sex offender Jeffrey Epstein and the trauma he inflicted on his young victims. When I was introduced to Sarah, the Duchess of York, in 2016 by a good friend and one of the most successful entrepreneurs you will never have heard of, and I then subsequently met the other members of the family, it was some time after the Duke's association with Epstein.

In the intervening years, I have provided advice to Sarah and the family on occasion. Through Sarah, I have met Prince Andrew and have always found him to be genuinely good company, if perhaps a bit detached and naïve in his outlook. He and Sarah had always been most hospitable, with various invitations to social engagements, which in turn led to informal meetings at Buckingham Palace and the Royal Lodge, Windsor. Our discussions often focused on the Fake Sheikh litigation that I handled on behalf of the Duchess, but other issues came up from time to time, including the escalating Epstein scandal.

In a professional career spanning more than forty years, I have never witnessed such an intense global onslaught on a person's reputation as that directed towards Prince Andrew. It is hard to think of a more dramatic example of a case that has been tried in the court of public opinion – as opposed to a court of law – and of the devastating impact that can follow.

The controversy around Prince Andrew's friendship with Jeffrey Epstein had been growing for years. He had been named in 2015 in court papers relating to Epstein, in which Virginia Giuffre claimed that she was forced to have sex with him. He has always vehemently denied all the allegations made against him. Occasionally, other equally famous and high-profile figures' names came up in relation to the scandal, but perhaps due to Prince Andrew's high profile and status as a senior member of the British Royal Family, this made him a more susceptible target.

I should make it clear at this point that although I have not been Prince Andrew's lawyer, the family are aware that I am writing this book and will be referencing them, but they have not sought to influence or interfere with anything I am writing here.

Roll on a couple of years to September 2019, when Prince Andrew invited me to meet him for a cup of tea when he was coming over to Northern Ireland to oversee the preparations for a forthcoming tournament at Royal Portrush Golf Club. I don't think he was looking for anything more than general chat and to follow up on a meeting I'd had with him and Sarah a couple of weeks earlier. Although not experiencing anything like the ferocious onslaught that was to come, he was at that time the subject of increasingly adverse coverage. On arrival at the golf club, I noticed a number of press photographers gathered at the perimeter fencing. Straight away, I realised that it would be no bad thing for Prince Andrew to be photographed with me. He was facing daily accusations and headlines in the press, and it was a chance to push back in actions if not words. The pictures would send out a message that he was minded to come out fighting against the allegations, encouraging the assumption that he had been consulting with me professionally for that reason, and perhaps discourage some of the more over-the-top and vexatious commentary.

I am not sure that the Duke understood where I was coming from when I made the suggestion that it might be helpful for us to be seen together in this context, but he certainly jumped at the opportunity to show me around the golf course and continue our discussion in the fresh Atlantic air. Prince Andrew came across to me as being very relaxed, notwithstanding the bank of photographers assembled a couple of hundred yards from where we were standing. It did not take too long for the cameras to start clicking and – in turn – the emails from journalists to begin to fill up my inbox. One Royal reporter called me expressing surprise that the Palace had not told him about the meeting, which must have been standard protocol. In due course, the Palace issued a statement saying that I had met with the Duke as 'a friend of the family'.

This engagement attracted national headlines – including 'Prince Andrew meets top libel lawyer Paul Tweed' (*The Times*), and 'Prince Andrew pictured with "fierce" top lawyer amid Jeffrey Epstein controversy' (*Daily Mirror*) – which achieved the desired effect in giving the impression that Prince Andrew was considering his legal options. When I met him at the Palace a few days later – to discuss an unrelated, private matter – he expressed astonishment and pleasure at the media coverage, which confirmed my opinion that he had not initially grasped the purpose of my strategy. In any event, he had some reprieve for several weeks, even if it was only temporary, from the more aggressive media headlines – at least until that disastrous *Newsnight* interview in November 2019.

I had been vaguely aware that Prince Andrew's private secretary, Amanda Thirsk, had been having discussions with the BBC for a period of months about the possibility of an interview with Emily Maitlis. I did not think for a moment that there was any possibility that this would go ahead – not least because of the firm advice of everyone close to him, including his ex-wife, urging him not to do it. However, out of the blue, in the week leading up to the broadcast, I received a call from Amanda Thirsk, who told me that Prince Andrew had decided to go ahead. When I expressed my absolute opposition, saying to Amanda that Prince Andrew definitely should not do it, she made her excuses, said that she would be in touch later and put the phone down abruptly.

That was the last I heard about the matter, but I nonetheless assumed that – with all the Palace and other advisors working in the background – someone would prevent the interview from taking place. It was so obviously an extremely bad idea. For Prince Andrew to expose himself to unrestricted cross-examination by a very expcricnced interviewer, who would have undertaken extensive research and prepared questions well in advance, could not possibly offer any upside in any circumstance to anyone. However, as the Duke was not my client, I was not in a position to be more forceful with my advice. When I heard that the interview had gone ahead, I couldn't believe it.

The one thing that this chain of events did make clear, to me at least, was that Prince Andrew believed himself to be innocent of the allegations against him, and that he also believed he could communicate that to the public.

I had been attending a family event in Scotland when the interview went out, so I couldn't watch it live. However, online media commentary and calls from colleagues left little doubt as to the inevitable and highly damaging fallout for the Duke, even though he himself had initially thought that the interview had gone quite well. However, his focus, demeanour and presentation were all wrong, probably due to his cocooned and protected upbringing, and the rest is history. He had given entirely the wrong impression during the interview – his failure to express regret for his friendship with Epstein and the fact that he didn't mention Epstein's victims or show any empathy for them led to the interview being described as a car crash.

I cannot help feeling that, while the strategy adopted on behalf of Prince Andrew post-*Newsnight* may have been deemed the right approach at the time in the context of possible criminal proceedings, it turned out to be unsuitable for dealing with the inevitable trial by media that he faced. A decision had been taken to concentrate on the perceived risk of criminal proceedings in the UK and to recruit a team of lawyers in anticipation of this happening. I took a different view – I could see that any legal battle was likely to take place on the other side of the Atlantic. I had, therefore, repeatedly emphasised that I believed it was vital to retain US counsel immediately, so that they could advise on and direct strategy there – where I knew the main exposure would be – while also managing the crucial media optics in both jurisdictions.

Unfortunately, the series of reactive public statements post-*Newsnight* did not work for such a high-profile matter in the public domain. The media optics of appearing to have the responses dragged out of you not only give the impression that you are on the back foot, but this reluctance can be misinterpreted as an attempt to conceal facts. While understanding the need for caution in the legal strategy, it was unfortunate that it came at the expense of structured and proactive media engagement. For instance, a carefully worded response, addressing all the facts together, could have been an option at the very outset.

The chosen strategy might have worked to some degree if Prince Andrew had adhered to the traditional Royal motto of 'never complain, never explain'. However, the minute the first denial statement was issued, he was immediately put in a position where it was believed necessary to issue subsequent reactionary statements. These did much to compound negative public perception, while encouraging the media to believe that there was a lot more to come. Unfortunately, these statements also all came across as defensive rather than proactive, and were extremely limited in their response, much to the frustration of at least one of the Duke's PR advisors at the time, who had been advocating for what I saw as a potentially much more effective approach to dealing with the mounting media pressure. Once the decision had been taken to engage and react, then a media strategy perhaps could and should have been implemented that took the initiative in terms of getting the facts out there, while explaining the Duke's stance.

My recommendations regarding the appointment of US attorneys – with appropriate experience and expertise, capable of dealing with both criminal and civil New York litigation protocols and the slightly more benign US media – had been taken up belatedly, with the retention of Blair Berk and Andrew Brettler. However, in the interim period, Ms Guiffre's attorneys had been given the time and opportunity to establish themselves in the driving seat of the litigation and the media optics, leaving the Duke's US legal team with an uphill struggle to regain lost ground.

While it may be unfair to pass judgement on decisions taken in what must have been very challenging circumstances, with immense pressure on the Duke coming from many quarters, it nonetheless appears to have been a mistake not to have engaged in negotiations with Virginia Giuffre's US attorney David Boies or to have replied to his correspondence. In my experience, without prejudice discussions with an opposite number have almost always borne some fruit for both parties, even if they have not led to a settlement. The advantages include establishing a line of direct contact with the decision makers; getting some idea of their stance and likely future tactics; and – if both lawyers have a genuine desire to bring matters to a head – the opportunity for terms to be agreed, which may not have appeared obvious previously. In the modern era, exposure to a full-blown court hearing poses a potential threat to a brand or reputation. To avoid recriminations being aired in court, many high-profile cases are resolved behind closed doors, often with substantial payments involved. On occasion, the payment of compensation is interpreted as an indication of fault – this is why the optics arising from a settlement are crucial. In the Duke's case, the challenge would have been to create an atmosphere and scenario where the complaint could be resolved on terms acceptable to both parties, while not necessarily making fundamental concessions on either side. This is where a carefully worded press release or statement read in open court comes into play, provided that there has not been too much reputational blood spilled in the preliminary sparring.

I was not involved in or even aware of the settlement negotiations that resulted in a significant financial payment in February 2022. Although this resolution may have been deemed necessary to avoid further distraction from the Queen's Platinum Jubilee, the timing, manner and general perception of the settlement could not have been worse for the Duke. It gave the clear impression that he was not only having to 'buy off' the claim, but additionally the size of the settlement payment also carried with it the inference that he was guilty of much of the alleged misconduct. The settlement resulted in nothing but negativity for him, in terms of the timing, the background and the amount, with his justification for why he was prepared to settle fading very much into the background. Whatever confidentiality had been agreed was completely ineffective in preventing immediate, and possibly ill-informed, speculation about the size of the settlement payment, with estimates ranging from $7m to $12m.

Matters had earlier been made much worse as a result of the perception that the Duke was attempting to avoid being personally served with the legal proceedings. Whatever the reason for this, it put him even further on the back foot. Certainly, there was nothing to be gained from ignoring the inevitability of eventual service.

Only the Duke, Virginia Giuffre, Ghislaine Maxwell and Epstein knew what did or did not happen at Maxwell's London abode and the extent of the Duke's involvement with Epstein. However, the price paid by the Duke in terms of the total devastation of his reputation, his loss of status within the Royal Family, his lack of options for the future, and the obvious financial implications could hardly have been higher.

In November 2022 it was reported that Virginia Giuffre had dropped a lawsuit naming the Harvard Law School Professor Alan Dershowitz, who she said had sexually assaulted her when she was a teenager, saying that she 'may have been mistaken'. Dershowitz's robust legal strategy clearly paid off and ultimately achieved the vindication of his reputation. The obvious question then is whether Prince Andrew might have achieved a similar outcome had he continued with his defence of the civil proceedings in the US, or whether the widely published photograph that shows him with Virginia Giuffre and Ghislaine Maxwell would have continued to be a blight on his case, regardless of its background circumstances. What is clear is that trial by media has, in the modern era, taken on a much greater significance than the traditional court hearing, disregarding the fundamental principle of a person being innocent until proven guilty. The impact of press reporting has been significantly exacerbated by social media and other internet forums, often rendering police investigations, never mind court deliberations, as seemingly almost of secondary importance. This change has come about largely due to the speed with which allegations are now disseminated to a worldwide audience, giving the impression that nobody is prepared to await the outcome of a criminal investigation or the completion of lengthy legal proceedings.

While this will have been apparent to those on the front line over the past number of years, it was a lesson made abundantly clear in the case of Prince Andrew. The finding of the court of public, and media, opinion can rarely be overturned by any appeal – whether in the form of legal action or following the belated revelation of subsequent information.

I have had experience over more than forty years of juries in operation, not only for defamation cases but also in the personal injury claims I worked on in the earlier years of my career. I have always found that the collective minds of a twelve- or seven-person jury (depending on the jurisdiction) will come to the right decision. The jury members have the benefit – and this is important – of hearing and assessing both adversaries in the witness box giving their evidence in person and also, crucially, under cross-examination. However, in the court of public opinion, the 'jury' members do not have the benefit of hearing all the evidence in this manner, and instead will be forming their opinions based on piecemeal information from one side or the other.

In Prince Andrew's case, no one heard his evidence as he would have given it in the witness box. In the *Newsnight* interview, he was not only unprepared and unfamiliar with how to best communicate the facts, or how to strike an empathetic pose, but he was further disadvantaged because in a court scenario most of his evidence would already have been submitted within detailed and documented pleadings, carefully prepared and discussed with his legal team. This would in turn have given him, as a lay person, an understanding of how to communicate the pertinent facts, which could have avoided the widespread misinterpretation and misunderstanding that followed the *Newsnight* interview. The court of public opinion has none of the legal protections built in to ensure a fair trial as in a court of law. The 'evidence' for the former tends to be based on media reports, preconceived perceptions and, sometimes, personal prejudice. Prince Andrew's *Newsnight* interview epitomises why I would not advise any of my clients, regardless of who they are or the strength of their case, to expose themselves in the way that he did.

In the years since the fateful interview, I have often wondered whether I could or should have done more to intervene. He could possibly have gained some advantage, at least in terms of media optics, say, if I had appeared at the Palace at the last minute and been seen to have dissuaded him from going ahead. He would have shown his willingness to open up about his involvement but in a way that suggested that this was being prevented by his lawyer.

Barney Eastwood, Paul Tweed and Barry Hearn signing the contract for the WBO Super-Middleweight Championship of the World third contest between Chris Eubank and Ray Close, 1995. (Courtesy of the Eastwood family)

Barry Hearn, Chris Eubank and Paul Tweed at the signing of the contract for the third contest between Eubank and Close. (Courtesy of the Eastwood family)

The Late Lord Brian Kerr, Baron Kerr of Tonaghmore (former Lord Chief Justice of Northern Ireland and Justice of the Supreme Court of the United Kingdom) with Paul Tweed outside our London office, 2010. (Courtesy of Paul Tweed)

Sharon Corr and Paul Tweed, the former a guest at the opening of our new London office, 2010. (Courtesy of Paul Tweed)

Uri Geller, Paul Tweed and Patrick Kielty at the opening of our new
London office, 2010. (Courtesy of Paul Tweed)

Gavin Bonner, Louis Walsh and Paul Tweed. Heading into court for Louis' legal action in the High Court in Dublin against the publishers of *The Sun*, 2012. (© PA Images/Alamy Stock Photo)

Another win for Ryanair! Outside the High Court in Belfast following the announcement of settlement with the *Irish Mail* with Ryanair Chief Pilot Captain Ray Conway and Ryanair Chief Executive Michael O'Leary, 2013. (© PA Images/Alamy Stock Photo)

Paul Tweed, Sarah Ferguson, Duchess of York, and Honorary Consul-General of Ireland M. Finbar Hill at the British American Business Council Los Angeles' 54th Annual Christmas Luncheon, 13 December 2013. (© John M. Heller/Getty Images)

Sarah Ferguson, Duchess of York, Paul Tweed, Selena Tweed and Princess Eugenie in the Royal Box at the George VI weekend at Royal Ascot, 2016. (© David Hartley/Shutterstock.com)

Paul and Selena Tweed at Windsor Castle as guests at the wedding of Princess Eugenie of York and Jack Brooksbank, 2018. (Courtesy of Paul Tweed)

Is Facebook Just a Platform? A Lawyer to the Stars Says No

By DAVID D. KIRKPATRICK

BELFAST, Northern Ireland — Paul Tweed made his name suing news organizations like CNN, Forbes and The National Enquirer on behalf of Hollywood movie stars, winning high-profile cases for celebrities like Britney Spears and Justin Timberlake by hopscotching among Belfast, London and Dublin to take advantage of their favorable defamation or privacy laws.

So it was telling last year when Mr. Tweed stopped by the Dublin office of a lawyer for Facebook, Twitter and other social media giants — many of which keep their non-United States headquarters in Ireland for tax reasons — with some half-playful questions.

Was public sentiment turning against the companies? Mr. Tweed wanted to know. Was a groundswell building over fake news, hate speech, revenge porn, online sex trafficking, defamation and privacy rights?

"It was odd," the Dublin lawyer, Richard Woulfe, recalled. "He wanted to sound me out, to find out my view on whether there were going to be more cases like this in the future."

Yes, indeed. Having enjoyed two decades of legal immunity on both sides of the Atlantic, social media giants are suddenly under growing pressure from regulators and lawmakers, especially in Europe. Lawyers are after them, too, filing lawsuits that seek to chip away at the legal protections affected the social media companies and to extract financial payments for defamation, privacy rights violations and data breaches.

Since the early years of the internet boom, American and European rules and regulations have deemed social media companies to be neutral "platforms" or "hosts," and thus immune from the liabilities faced by traditional publishers. But a series of scandals over their content has put the companies under a new assault — and the broad question of whether they should be seen as publishers rather than agnostic platforms

the online publication Middle East Eye, as well as Facebook and Twitter, over allegations that he participated in an attempted coup in Turkey.

Over the past year, Mr. Tweed said, he has also handled more than 20 cases involving so-called revenge porn — the posting on social media of sexually explicit images of a former lover, one of the most politically sensitive issues for the companies. He declined to disclose how many had ended in financial settlements, citing confidentiality agreements.

Then, in January, another Belfast lawyer reached a settlement with Facebook in a case about the posting online in 2014 of naked photographs of a 14-year-old girl, which reappeared repeatedly even after her family had asked Facebook to remove them. Facebook agreed to a financial payment, which typically would include a confidentiality agreement. Her lawyer, nevertheless, told local journalists in a brief statement that the settlement "moves the goal posts."

"It now puts the onus on the provider to look at how they respond to indecent, abusive and other such images put on their platform," the lawyer, Pearse MacDermott, said at the time. "Had those images been put in a newspaper or on TV there would be serious repercussions."

Mr. Tweed, under no confidentiality agreement, spoke out about the significance of the case and now represents the victim. In a February debate over revenge porn televised on the Irish national broadcaster, Mr. Tweed squared off against Niamh Sweeney, Facebook's policy chief for Ireland. Ms. Sweeney said that one way Facebook was trying to address the issue was by inviting individuals to preemptively submit naked or other embarrassing pictures of themselves so the company's software could block efforts to post the images. (A pilot program is underway in Australia.)

Absurd, Mr. Tweed countered in a later interview. Was would Face-

Paul Tweed, top, in Dublin in 2014, after settling a case for Justin Timberlake and his wife, Jessica Biel. Above left, Sri Lankan soldiers in Digana's March, after Facebook linked abuse. Above right, the office of Facebook's lawyer in central London.

Making the news stateside. From *The New York Times*. (© 2018 The New York Times Company. All rights reserved. Used under license.)

Prince Andrew, Duke of York, with Paul Tweed, 2019. This was the moment the Duke got my strategy! (© PA Images/Alamy Stock Photo)

Paul Tweed and David Ringland KC. Outside the High Court in Belfast following the record damages award to former NI First Minister Arlene Foster, 2021. (© Stephen Hamilton/Press Eye)

Law Society of Northern Ireland Centenary Panel discussion 2022 supported by several of my well-known clients: Stephen Nolan, Miriam O'Callaghan, Graham Ogilvy, Brigid Napier (President of the Law Society of Northern Ireland) and Louis Walsh.
(Courtesy of the Law Society of Northern Ireland)

EIGHT

You Can't Put the Genie Back in the Bottle

W hen it comes to social media, the slow progress of litigation is in stark contrast to the high speed with which a defamatory tweet, fake ad or piece of malicious misinformation can spread around the world. The reckless tweeting of defamatory comments has been the subject of numerous warnings and also extensive litigation, with serious financial consequences. Several cases I have brought on behalf of clients in recent times have resulted in substantial damages awards or settlements, with the defendant liable to pay not only their own legal costs but those of the plaintiff as well, as costs are normally awarded as a matter of course to the winning side.

On 23 December 2019, Harley Street doctor and television personality Dr Christian Jessen, tweeted to his more than 300,000 followers that NI First Minister Arlene Foster had been having an extra-marital affair. Not only was the tweet and false allegation extremely distressing for Mrs Foster, but the timing made matters even worse. The fact that we were so close to Christmas also presented a problem for me. Our office was closing for the holiday period, and, with limited resources available and the absence of any means of contacting Jessen directly, I was left with the dilemma of having to decide whether or not I should risk further dissemination of the defamatory allegation by issuing a warning to Jessen in an open, public tweet.

Having discussed this with my client, and in light of the ongoing damage being caused to her, we decided that there was little alternative, and I proceeded accordingly. This resulted in the inevitable social media jibes, mainly directed at Mrs Foster but some also aimed at me. A number of social media would-be lawyers claimed that my tweeted notice to Jessen did no more than cause a 'Barbra Streisand effect' – generating even more publicity for the offending allegation than it had received in the first place. My tweet was also and perhaps inevitably picked up by the media, leading to a headline BBC news item on Christmas Day.

Jessen did not react immediately to my warning. When he did respond, it was with 'LOL' (Laugh Out Loud), and it took him another two weeks to delete his original tweet. This set the tone for the months to come. While I am well used to provocative responses, I felt very bad for Mrs Foster, who was genuinely upset about the embarrassment that had been inflicted on her family and had to face her fellow parishioners at church over the Christmas period. Although she is a hardened and very experienced politician, this was difficult for her to bear.

In spite of the initial negativity from Jessen and the absence of immediate legal remedies, the client placed her full confidence in me and showed incredible backbone driving forward the litigation, which is always an unpredictable process.

Jessen made matters worse at every cut and turn by ignoring subsequent emails and correspondence, including the service of a Writ of Summons and follow-up pleadings. He appeared to be unrepentant throughout and, to his cost, continued to ignore my urging that he place the matter in the hands of his own solicitor. This resulted in us obtaining what is known as a 'Judgment in Default', leaving only the question of compensation to be assessed and determined by the court. However, before we got to that final stage, Jessen woke up to the serious position his arrogance had put him in. At the last minute he instructed solicitors to try to get the judgment set aside, with a view to belatedly attempting to contest the matter. Despite the fact that, in my opinion, he really didn't have a leg to stand on in terms of argument and had exacerbated damage by failing to apologise or even discuss the libel at an early stage, the trial judge, Mr Justice McAlinden, showed considerable patience in allowing him to put his case to the court.

Jessen appeared to be unrepentant right to the end, at least so far as my client and I were concerned. Rather than apologise, even at this late stage, he began to throw money at his defence and brought in a leading London senior counsel. Although it was difficult to assess or predict how the trial judge was viewing this strategy, it was quite clear from my experience in these matters that the judge was allowing Jessen and his legal team every conceivable opportunity to put their case before the court in order to minimise the chance of there being any grounds for an appeal.

On 27 May 2021, Arlene Foster was awarded £125,000 at the High Court in Belfast, which was record damages for a tweet. There were a number of aggravating factors, not least the apparent contempt Dr Jessen had for Mrs Foster – and for me personally – never mind his failure to apologise for the embarrassment and distress inflicted on her. The case was also significant in that it was heard by a judge sitting without a jury. Sometimes, a jury is accused of getting it wrong due to bias or a failure to grasp the legal issues and consequences, or losing the plot when it comes to assessing the level of damages. Mr Justice McAlinden based his findings in this case on a careful, comprehensive and analytical assessment of the evidence, leading to a very detailed and reasoned judgment. Unsurprisingly, Dr Jessen thought better of lodging an appeal.

Lawyers usually adopt a thick-skinned approach when it comes to personal criticism from the opposition in this type of case. However, Dr Jessen's conduct was so provocative and out of order – from his 'LOL' reply to my initial tweeted warning to the fact that he appeared to have disregarded many of my subsequent communications – I am afraid that I could not help but comment to the media outside the court after the judgment had been handed down, that 'I don't think he's laughing now!' More importantly, this six-figure award together with costs had provided not only a long overdue precedent, but also a warning to anyone who believed that they could tweet with impunity.

Another Twitter user faced the consequences of their actions a little later the same year. BBC presenter and independent producer Stephen Nolan, who is a longstanding client of mine, had been subjected to vicious trolling on social media for some time, not least because of the contentious nature of his very popular television and radio programmes, which encourage debate – often heated – on the current issues affecting Northern Ireland. One anonymous Twitter user, posting as 'Pastor Jimberoo', was unrelenting in seeking to undermine and ridicule him. Pastor Jimberoo had not bargained on Stephen's tenacity and determination.

It is normally almost impossible to find out who is behind an anonymous account without a court order, but, with the help of a private investigator, Stephen managed to track down and identify the person, enabling me to follow up with a robust legal notice. The user immediately realised that he had a serious problem on his hands, not least because his own reputation and employment were now at risk. He immediately put his hands up, through his solicitor, and effectively bought his anonymity with a six-figure settlement. An expensive lesson, and he was fortunate that Nolan – satisfied that a sufficient example had been made of him – was magnanimous enough to allow him to remain anonymous. Several other tweeters who had received warning letters from us immediately followed suit and settled, though for more modest financial payments. The combined outcome in favour of Stephen Nolan has acted as a deterrent, not only in protecting him but also many other victims of this type of malicious trolling. The six-figure settlement made headlines across Ireland and subsequently was the subject of a number of newspaper and magazine features. All this acted as a reminder, and a warning, that any cloak of online anonymity can be removed. These cases combined to show that it is vital to think carefully before tweeting or re-tweeting, and that malicious tweets can result in a very serious financial penalty.

It is not only members of the general public who need to take heed of such risks, but also journalists. In recent times there has been a tendency for reporters to tweet headlines with links to their published articles. In defamation law an article, including the headline, has to be read and taken as a whole. In other words, a headline may contain a defamatory imputation, but if the position is explained properly and accurately in the body of the article, this will be taken as negating any adverse inferences, thereby defeating any potential libel claim. I have always been conscious of the unfairness of what I believe to be a legal anomaly: the fact that the front page of a paper, sitting in a prominent place on a newsstand, can often be the only part that the general public sees or bothers to read. The content of the actual article is totally overlooked. In tweeting merely a headline, journalists risk losing the defence of the article having to be taken as a whole. This exposure can increase further, if an additional defamatory comment accompanies the retweeted article. In other words, if only the headline is republished with no mitigating explanation or justification, then it can be taken, in certain circumstances, as a standalone, potentially defamatory comment.

I have always emphasised this hazard to my journalist clients, as it is becoming increasingly common for a reporter's tweet to be included in any substantive legal proceedings against the publisher of a newspaper or periodical. It is an approach that I have had to employ reluctantly myself on behalf of several complainants. Unfortunately, through lack of understanding of the law, many journalists do not appreciate this subtle distinction, whereby liability is assessed on what they have put within *their* tweet, even if they have included a link to the article. It doesn't help that articles are not always readily accessible and can be behind a pay wall. The general advice therefore applies to my journalist clients as well: always think before you tweet, and assess the tweet in the narrowest context.

Newspaper owners can face similar, indirect exposure from the readers' comment sections under online articles. In other words, the comments underneath an online article should be treated no differently to a reader's letter in a print edition, which is expected to be carefully vetted by a newspaper editor before being approved for publication. To my mind, there should be no difference between a publisher's responsibility for online comments and a social media company's liability for a user's postings, subject to appropriate notice and an opportunity being afforded to remove the offending words. Google, Facebook *et al.* continue to repeat their mantra that they are merely a platform and not a publisher. I have been asked many times how they can keep maintaining what is, in my opinion, a totally untenable and increasingly ludicrous position. They are now responsible for a significant proportion of news dissemination across the world and also divert advertising revenue from mainstream media, while benefiting from expensive investigative journalism often without a corresponding payment. In other words, they are getting all the benefits and all the rewards without any of the associated responsibilities.

One of the most common scenarios that my firm comes across arises from a reckless tweet or social media post in which an allegation made during an employment tribunal hearing is exaggerated or distorted by one of the parties – some participants lose the run of themselves in their desire to strike back at the employer. They do not realise that in making such assertions, they have lost the protection of legal privilege and are therefore potentially subject to legal challenge. Quite often, a disaffected employee will be just as dissatisfied with the progress of the tribunal proceedings as they had been with their employer's purported treatment of them. This impatience can sometimes result in them running to their social media accounts to vent their frustration and fury. A foolish mistake.

As I have repeatedly emphasised, users should always be conscious of the need to think and pause before tweeting or posting, bearing in mind that a comment can reach thousands of followers before a mistake is even realised, never mind remedied. It should also be remembered that the deletion of a tweet or a post is not the end of the matter – most savvy users know to take a screenshot when an offending tweet is brought to their attention at the outset. I have found on many occasions that even unrepentant tweeters, such as Christian Jessen, will discreetly take down an offending tweet, hoping that will be the end of the matter. However, most of the dissemination will have taken place within hours, if not minutes, of the posting.

Although it is Twitter, now X, that has been the focus of many complaints in the past, Facebook and another Meta subsidiary, Instagram, have had their share of legal attention. Not only does Facebook have increased exposure as a result of facilitating the republication of newspaper articles, but its users frequently go over the top in terms of verbal abuse, harassment and other unsavoury conduct. While Facebook, like Twitter/X, has traditionally tried to pass the buck on to the offending user, as I am constantly repeating, the days of the 'merely a platform' or innocent dissemination argument should be long gone and certainly no longer acceptable in any society.

In the past, several platforms have also had a standard policy of notifying a user upon receipt of a removal request concerning content on that account. Whether intentional or not, this policy can act to deter people from coming forward with a complaint – in the case of trolls, this kind of complaint is more likely to increase or highlight their campaign than stop them. To make matters worse, some social media platforms often indicate that they will provide a redacted copy of the complaint to notify Lumen, a central database that provides details of specific complaints against the social media companies, leading to further dissemination, which represents yet another deterrence to people coming forward to complain. As Stephen Nolan discovered, most of the platforms are not so forthcoming when it comes to identifying anonymous users, for what they claim to be data protection reasons.

This refusal is increasingly significant as we move into the era of AI. I have never understood nor accepted the platform's so-called principled stance in refusing to identify anonymous posters in the absence of a court order requiring them to do so. Bearing in mind that an application for such an order is likely to cost a very significant five-figure sum (the applicant is usually responsible for both sets of costs, successful or not), this option is outside the financial reach of most people. The legislators have shown a persistent reluctance to intervene, particularly in the US, and show no signs of changing their stance any time soon.

NINE

Battling on Either Side of the Atlantic

The past couple of years have still seen a number of high-profile libel actions, in spite of the persistent attempts by legislators to discourage defamation actions, or at least to lower damages awards by removing juries from the equation. While the media's criticism in the past has focused on the scale of damages awarded and on overseas litigants utilising the UK and Irish courts, there is much less discussion of the overall financial implications arising from significantly increased legal costs, with no sign of the number of defamation actions abating. Indeed quite the contrary.

Even in that bastion of free speech, the US, where the First Amendment protections traditionally make it very difficult to bring libel proceedings, there have been enormous damages awards and settlements in recent times. On the other hand, awards in the UK have gradually fallen in tandem with the legislation that was introduced with that objective in mind, but legal costs have gone through the roof, as an addition to damages. In the US the costs are normally taken from the compensation. In other words, in the US the award is representative of the actual cost and value of the case, whereas in England damages are now only a fraction of the total financial exposure.

Johnny Depp and Amber Heard's legal battles – in London in 2020 and in Virginia, USA, in 2022 – have been among the most high profile. In the London case, Johnny Depp sued the publishers of *The Sun* for labelling him 'a wife beater'. The outcome was nothing short of a disaster for him – the judge said that the newspaper had proved that what was in the article was 'substantially true'. In the immediate aftermath, Warner Bros asked Depp to resign from playing the role of Gellert Grindelwald in the Harry Potter spin-off film series *Fantastic Beasts*. Depp survived to fight a rematch on the other side of the Atlantic in Virginia, in the equivalent of a high-stakes poker match with the world watching in what seemed like gleeful anticipation. In this case, Depp alleged that a column about domestic violence that Heard had written for the *Washington Post* had defamed him and asked for $50 million in damages. Heard filed a countersuit for $100 million.

The case turned into a social media shitstorm: it was one of the first big celebrity cases to play out on the platforms. The coverage could not have been described as being in any way impartial. TikTok took the lead in facilitating a deluge of offensive comment aimed primarily at Amber Heard, with every aspect of her evidence being scrutinised, recreated and ridiculed. Even though TikTok, in common with most of the other platforms, has guidelines aimed at removing abusive content amounting to harassment, threats or attempts to mock, humiliate or embarrass, they seemed either unable or unwilling to deal with the tsunami of abuse they were publishing.

More than twenty-five years earlier, in 1995, people were glued to their TV screens when O.J. Simpson was on trial for the murders of his ex-wife, Nicole Brown Simpson, and her friend Ronald Goldman. As many as 150 million people tuned in to watch the moment when the verdict was announced. By the time of the *Depp v Heard* case, the interest had migrated on to the social media platforms, and the opinions of TikTokkers seemed to overtake rational assessment by experts.

For two people very much accustomed to dealing with the media, it was perhaps surprising that they chose to seek vindication in the courts, which were unfamiliar territory for both of them, rather than using the media or social media to put across their sides of the story. In the first instance, in London, this decision proved to be a total disaster for Johnny Depp, where the judge sitting without a jury analysed the legal factors and came to his decision based strictly and entirely on the evidence presented to him. When it came to the second round of the litigation, taking place in the US, not only was it a jury determining the case, but the court of *social media* opinion was giving its verdict even before the jury had a chance to consider all the evidence. When it was time for the jury to reach their decision, it fell in line with the almost unanimous views expressed on the various platforms.

Johnny was awarded $10 million in compensatory damages and $5 million in punitive damages (reduced to $350,000 in accordance with the state limit), and Amber was awarded $2 million with the finding that a former Depp attorney had defamed her. It was reported that Johnny Depp ultimately settled for $1 million donated to charity.

I had acted for the couple back in 2015, when they appeared to be happily married – my brief contact with them gave no indication of what was to come. I managed to secure several apologies from the tabloids in relation to articles making inaccurate allegations about their marriage and a controversy involving their dogs on a trip to Australia. What a difference a few years, or just a few months, can make!

However, just when the general public and the tabloids thought that the Depp–Heard cases could not be bettered in terms of celebrity gossip and drama, along came the Wagatha Christie case. The litigation brought the private lives and social habits of footballers' wives and B-List celebrities into focus, and the prospect of what would emerge had even the seasoned red-top reporters gasping in gleeful anticipation. It was a tabloid editor's dream, never mind a lawyers' benefit match. The public generally have an insatiable appetite for celebrity gossip, regardless of who it involves or where it has come from, but getting it from the witness box provides an aura of authenticity, not to mention legal protection, for those passing it on.

In 2019 Coleen Rooney – married to footballer Wayne Rooney – announced on social media that the source for leaks from her private Instagram stories to *The Sun* had been Rebekah Vardy's account. In 2020 Vardy, wife of footballer Jamie Vardy, sued Rooney for libel, and the case came to court in May 2022. In July of the same year, the judge ruled in Rooney's favour, and dismissed the case against her.

A lesson to be learned from the *Vardy v Rooney* case is the importance of thinking very carefully before embarking on the intense and highly stressful process of bringing a libel action. Once committed, it is very difficult to extract yourself unless there is a degree of co-operation from your opposite number, however reluctant. The Wagatha Christie case is a prime example of the difficulty of getting off the libel rollercoaster once you are on it and gives credence to the popular analogy that continuing to dig only makes a hole much bigger. All the while, the legal costs register is pinging at an alarming rate.

I always tell my clients that they should be litigating with a view to vindicating their reputation rather than hoping for a financial windfall. This is why most of the cases I handle are settled in the early stages, with a pragmatic approach taken by both sides. Putting on my defence hat, this makes sense in that the real financial hazard for a publisher on the back foot is their exposure to significantly increasing legal costs with every week that goes by. Likewise, as time is of the absolute essence in most cases, it is far more sensible for a plaintiff to settle quickly for a comprehensive and prominent apology, which can be disseminated back down the internet at the outset, rather than having to wait for anything up to two years for vindication in the courts.

* * *

The costs in the Rooney-Vardy litigation will have been eye-watering, with the losing party left with a bill running into millions of pounds, and even the winning side having some level of financial exposure. The court or taxing master in the UK will usually only grant recovery in the region of 70 per cent of the total costs claimed, the remainder being regarded as a solicitor and client fee, which still has to be borne by the 'winning' party, although in the Wagatha Christie case the court ordered that Vardy should pay 90 per cent of Rooney's costs. As the saying goes, the libel courts are not for widows and orphans: with legal costs often coming in at £2 to £3 million for each side, the level of damages is of secondary consideration.

The US legal system differs from England in terms of offering a trial by jury; another difference is that costs do not normally follow the event. Instead, the plaintiff's attorneys will often enter into a contingency arrangement with their client. These arrangements mean that the attorneys receive a large proportion of the damages awarded, in return for financing the costs of the litigation, if the case goes their way. They obviously also take the risk that, if they lose, they could end up with the substantial costs incurred from running the case and no damages. This system takes a considerable degree of pressure off a plaintiff because if they lose their legal action, at least they will not have to pay their lawyers' fees. It also means that the attorney has to assess a case very carefully before taking it on. They have to factor in their own hours, expert reports (such as jury advisors and PR consultants) and other outlay as the case progresses, with no guarantee of getting a return. Accordingly, it is really not too difficult for many attorneys to justify a potential contingency fee of up to 40 per cent of the damages awarded.

I am sure that Rebekah Vardy would have preferred to have had the option of bringing her libel action against Coleen Rooney in the US where she would have had the benefit of the different costs scenario, rather than having to pay all her own lawyers' fees together with the bulk of costs of her opponent's legal team.

Another striking recent case is the high-profile defamation action filed by Dominion Voting Systems against Fox News in March 2021. In the weeks after President Trump lost the 2020 election, a number of Fox News interviewees claimed to have evidence that voter fraud was to blame. That evidence never emerged, but accusations were directed towards Dominion, a manufacturer of election technology whose algorithms – the news channel claimed – 'were designed to be inaccurate'. Dominion took action against Fox, claiming that they had been defamed as a result of the TV station broadcasting lies about its machines.

Sections of the US media described the libel action as one of the most extraordinary brought against an American media company in more than a generation. The case also stood out because it involved multiple false statements and on account of the sheer scale of the damages claimed – US$1.6 billion. Although the case didn't go to trial, Dominion's stance was vindicated by Fox's payment of a last-minute settlement of $787.5 million. The story didn't end there. Dominion also had actions pending against other stations that broadcast similar content as well as against a number of Trump allies, including Rudy Giuliani, who appeared on the media outlets to spread and repeat these untruths.

The scale of recent awards in the US wholly contradicts the perception that the US is a no-go jurisdiction for defamation claims – an American branch office is a very attractive prospect ... if only in my imagination!

In my experience, although the US has a much more defendant-friendly approach to libel actions, to make up for this, there is also a much stricter culture with regard to fact checking before publication. This is not limited to putting questions to the subject of the article. Rather, editors put their journalists under pressure to ensure the accuracy of their story. In the UK and Ireland, as long as the questions are put to the subject of the story – and regardless of how late in the day this occurs – an editor can sometimes see this as the discharge of their journalistic obligations.

The US publications tend not only to have a more cautious and considered approach, but also to take their time before running with a story. By contrast, in the UK and Ireland, there is an often an urgency, with the aim of getting an exclusive scoop out before competitors. This can increase the likelihood of mistakes occurring.

Another anomaly between litigation in the US and the UK/Ireland is the extent of the discovery process. Discovery is the legal term for exchange of relevant documents between the parties. In the UK, correspondence between a client and his lawyer has always been privileged and excluded from the discovery process. Not so in the US, where a lawyer's written advice to a client is open to scrutiny in many circumstances, which is certainly good reason for a lawyer to be cautious in their advice.

I was exposed to this scenario when advising a very successful businesswoman, who although born in Northern Ireland, had established an international oil company based in the US. Without going into any of the detail of the litigation in that jurisdiction, to my shock and surprise, the power and reach of the US courts extended to Ireland, with the High Court being asked to consider an application for access to my email advice to my client, which would have been discoverable under US law. Needless to say, this has led me to adopt an extremely cautious and circumspect approach in advising my clients in writing ever since!

In spite of all this, my client bases continued to expand over the years, the extent of which can be epitomised in the recent Trump hush money trial. In the increasingly small media world in which we now live, totally independently of each other I have provided advice to Keith Davidson, the attorney who has been in the firing line in the witness box in the court in New York giving evidence regarding monies allegedly paid to his client, Stormy Daniels.

Against the background of the same trial, I have also in the past provided advice to Dylan Howard, the former editor of the *National Enquirer*, who gave his evidence pre-trial before a grand jury and was regarded as another key witness in the indictment case against Donald Trump. In another Trump-related matter, I have also in the distant past provided some informal guidance to one of his former wives.

Such is the global village and the nature of the work I undertake, that these overlapping connections have been happening more and more.

TEN

Conspiracy and Disinformation

B ack in the day, most people who peddled conspiracy theories were treated as crackpots and had no credibility – many of those involved in far-fetched speculation found their careers suddenly grinding to a halt as their personal credibility disappeared out the window. Many bizarre and fabricated stories were often sensationalised in the likes of the *National Enquirer* and other supermarket tabloids, and were ignored by almost everyone. The advent of social media has changed all that. Conspiracy theories can now spread rapidly and on multiple platforms. Bots, trolls and social media users can share information and propaganda at the click of a mouse. A report from the FBI in 2019 cited conspiracy theories as a new domestic terror threat, potentially driving extremists to carry out criminal or violent acts.

Most conspiracy theories over the past couple of years have focused on the pandemic, emanating primarily from the anti-vax movement. The theories, largely aimed at government, gathered great pace and were afforded significant credibility, not least due to the volume and international scale of the commentary. This led to the tragic consequences of hospital beds being taken up largely by the unvaccinated, who had fallen victim to the many unsubstantiated rumours circulating on social media. It was the hospitals and health workers around the world who had to pay the heavy price, and there will continue to be a devastating knock-on impact on the treatment of the sick and elderly for many years to come. We will probably never know the full extent of the avoidable illness and deaths caused by certain sections of the anti-vax propaganda.

These theories also put increased pressure on politicians around the world, with their credibility already under considerable scrutiny and often under attack. People did not know who or what to believe, particularly in the early days while the pandemic was at its height. These conspiracy theories were weaponised by keyboard warriors to undermine health advisors around the world, and even those philanthropists who had been investing their own money in an attempt to improve the vaccine situation.

The people who believe in these theories see them as facts that the mainstream media are afraid to report on. According to several studies, the likes of Facebook, YouTube and TikTok outperformed mainstream news sources when it came to Covid-related news. The underlying trend is a certain distrust of the mainstream media, meaning that the social media platforms are a breeding ground for many outrageous theories. Social media is now at the forefront as a source of news, particularly for the younger generation. Not only do the social media companies amplify and recommend posts and videos, but they afford the theories a significant degree of credibility that would not otherwise exist.

However, while the protagonists in the anti-vax lobby have been left largely unchallenged, two ground-breaking jury awards against the high-profile conspiracy theorist Alex Jones finally afforded an opportunity not only to punish Jones, but to send out a warning that a US jury will be prepared to impose a serious financial sanction in response to the malicious spread of disinformation.

On 14 December 2012, a young man in Connecticut killed his mother and then travelled to Sandy Hook Elementary School where he shot dead twenty children, all aged six and seven, and six adults. Before long, conspiracy theories began to spread online about what had happened, the main thrust of them being that the massacre had been staged as a part of a government plot to introduce gun control. Within hours of the shooting, Alex Jones was giving voice to such theories, claiming that it had been a drill, that the victims were still alive and that the parents were 'crisis actors' paid by the government. Having suffered years of abuse, the parents of one of the children massacred at Sandy Hook sued Jones and were awarded $49 million in damages by a Texas judge in 2022.

This case was followed a few weeks later by an award from a Connecticut jury of almost $1 billion in damages to eight other families and an FBI agent who was one of the first on the scene after the shooting. Although Jones remained largely unrepentant, and the prospects for recovery of the full sum had been remote, the size of this award will have sent another warning, not only to those peddling conspiracy theories but also to the social media platforms. Even they must have been feeling nervous twinges of concern at this level of damages, notwithstanding their enormous financial war chests and the perceived protection offered by Section 230 of the Communications Decency Act in the US. This Act has been interpreted as giving the online platforms total protection from any liability for what has been posted on their sites. The protection provided by this legislation is significant, and explains in part why Jones still had access to Facebook and YouTube as recently as 2018, some six years after he began his ranting over the Sandy Hook tragedy. Even then, Facebook had initially implemented nothing more than a four-week suspension. Although the main conduit for Jones's malicious theories had been his own Infowars website and other related sites, where he also sells his merchandise, Facebook, YouTube and other platforms had also been, to all intents and purposes, facilitating him and many other conspiracy theorists.

The families had reportedly been subjected to death threats, and had their personal information, including their addresses, posted online, forcing them to move away from their homes as they struggled to come to terms with their tragic losses. One of the parents – Jeremy Richman, a neuroscientist – had not only taken a defamation case himself, but for a number of years he delivered lectures and met with community groups, all with the aim of ensuring that others would not suffer in the way that he and his family had suffered. By doing so, and within days of his daughter's murder, he became a target for the conspiracy theorists. Dr Richman took his own life in 2019, seven years after losing his daughter. Alex Jones put out a message of condolence, but hours later questioned whether his suicide was just another hoax.

Throughout this period, Jones's Sandy Hook conspiracy tirade attracted millions of like-minded listeners, who were then bombarded with ads for his testosterone supplements and other products he was promoting. Just before he was banned by YouTube, Apple, Facebook, Spotify and Twitter in 2018, Jones apparently sold $800,000 worth of merchandise each day. What is even more disturbing is not only the number of followers Jones had on YouTube and other platforms, but the fact that he attracted an enormous volume of comments, most of which were in support of his views.

It is difficult to imagine more offensive conduct. Jones was also the cheerleader for an army of trolls who had jumped on his bandwagon. It wasn't until midway through the first trial that he was forced to admit that he had fabricated his claims, and to accept that this was a real-life tragedy. However, it was only intense cross-examination that extracted this admission. As to whether Jones will demonstrate any degree of genuine repentance has been open to doubt: he instructed his lawyer to apply for a mistrial on numerous occasions, while condemning the jury as stooges and the hearing as a show trial.

Online trolling of this nature is not restricted to the US. There have been similar attacks in England. For example, families and survivors of the Manchester Arena attack, in which twenty-two people were killed, have been accused of acting by online trolls, with a conspiracy theorist admitting to filming them to 'see if injuries were real'.

Another example has been a harassment campaign during which 'gamergaters' created conspiracy theories co-ordinated into a misogynistic, right-wing backlash against feminism and diversity. Gamergate targeted women in the video game industry with rape and death threats, alleging collusion between the press and feminists.

In August 2022 after many months of alleged mis-information breaches, Facebook and Instagram belatedly decided to remove Robert Kennedy Jr's group, for 'repeatedly' violating their guidelines by spreading medi-cal misinformation and anti-vaccine dogma. Why it had taken Facebook so long to take this action is difficult to understand or justify, and removing the account several years down the line, after the pandemic had largely run its course, made this academic, if not pointless, after all the damage had been done.

Conspiracy theorists also regurgitate and re-energise historic stories, with theories surrounding the death of Princess Diana coming to the fore again. Many of these instances of misinformation include some factual references, which give more authenticity to fake elements of the story, and which in turn give further legs to the much vaunted 'fake news'. A blatant example was a series of fake ads supported by false bots, suggesting that my client, Miriam O'Callaghan, was marketing a face cream and that – as a result of this controversy – she had lost her job with Ireland's national broadcaster. No face cream company existed, but people were still transferring money to this fraudulent operation, believing they were buying a face cream endorsed by Miriam. Having exhausted all other avenues, she consulted me with a view to taking legal action to force Facebook to remove the offending 'ads'. The combination of fact and fabrication afforded sufficient credibility for lots of people to be duped – due to Miriam's reputation as a high-profile television presenter, the idea of her advertising a genuine product of this nature was not beyond the bounds of credibility.

A separate question when going back to the motivation of conspiracy theorists is whether or not they believe what they are alleging. In Jones's case, Scarlett Lewis, whose six-year-old son Jesse was killed in the Sandy Hook school tragedy, formed a view after facing Jones down in August 2022 that he did not believe the falsehoods that he had been spreading, and the fact that he had been making copious sums of money from his stance provides an obvious motive for his actions.

The problem for the social media and video platforms is that they are facing an increasingly inventive user base, who have learned many tricks of the trade to get their messages of hate and violence across without triggering any of the preventive controls that have been put in place.

The controversies surrounding James 'the Ayatollah' Owens, who amassed a global fan base with his racist messages, are a case in point. The protagonist, a journalism graduate, utilised euphemisms and code words in order to wrong-foot YouTube's AI warning system. Although he had attempted to conceal his identity, *The Times* investigations editor unmasked him in a September 2022 article. I am firmly of the view that YouTube, having provided the platform and the means for this type of racist hate speech to be disseminated, should accept responsibility regardless of the challenges faced in policing this type of misuse.

There is also an overlap between conspiracy theories and hate speech, with both having a devastating effect. In December 2021 a large group of Rohingya refugees initiated legal action against Facebook in the UK and the US, accusing the social media platform of allowing hate speech against them to spread. They had been seeking more than $150 billion in compensation, claiming Facebook's platforms promoted violence against the persecuted minority.

These legal complaints are significant in that they are being brought on either side of the Atlantic and are no doubt a sign of things to come for the platforms. A number of the allegations against Facebook in this case have included claims that Facebook's algorithms 'amplified hate speech against the Rohingya people'; that Facebook failed to invest in moderators and fact-checkers who actually knew about the political situation in Myanmar; and that they failed to take down posts inciting violence against Rohingya. Facebook has more than 20 million users in Myanmar, with the site often being the only way of obtaining and disseminating news there. Thousands of people have died, and a massive refugee crisis has unfolded, with many Rohingya fleeing to Bangladesh and widespread allegations of human rights and other abuses. Unfortunately, the action brought by the Rohingya was dismissed by a court in California, but it did highlight the power and reach of Facebook, if not their accountability.

Many clients who come to us have had malicious allegations published about them online. They are shocked by how challenging it is to achieve a quick, positive response to a complaint to social media giants, and on many occasions how difficult it is to get them to take the disinformation down. In recent times the most common complaints from our clients have been centring on malicious allegations that have been published about them online with the sole intention of causing harm or embarrassment. I have had to deal with trolls spreading disinformation about clients, in the knowledge and with the intention of creating problems for the target with their banking arrangements or political ambitions. The reluctance on the part of some online platforms to intervene and suspend an account, other than in exceptional circumstances, makes these problems difficult to resolve. Some frustrated clients have even speculated as to a possible degree of political or other influence in that decision-making process. Regardless of whether such factors are actually in the background or not, the immense power and control wielded by online conglomerates is indisputable.

These kinds of allegations constitute disinformation – false information disseminated for a malicious and calculated purpose. Disinformation is intended to discredit, defame, and possibly incite others by fomenting conspiracy theories or affording credibility to fabricated allegations. (By contrast, misinformation is false information shared due to a genuine mistake or misunderstanding, maybe unwittingly or even with good intentions.)

When clients come to us with their complaints, they often express exasperation when I tell them that the platforms cannot be compelled to take down the offending content on the first request, and that it often takes legal proceedings to get their attention. This unsatisfactory state of affairs is made worse by a number of apparently random takedowns that are implemented with no consistency or obvious common denominator.

These complaints are therefore an uphill struggle for us from the outset. The minute a fabricated report appears in the online stratosphere, it can be disseminated within seconds and it is virtually impossible to undo the damage, at least in the short term. Arlene Foster's case was a prime example of this, even with Twitter's subsequent co-operation, although she is only one of many victims I have represented over the years. Thankfully most could be dealt with surgically at an early stage and before there was extensive public dissemination. Unfortunately, the higher the profile of the person concerned, the more interest in the offending tweet or post and the more rapidly it is disseminated into the online stratosphere. The victim is then left with the daunting prospect of having to issue legal proceedings quickly, with an accompanying press statement, which in turn runs the risk of creating that 'Barbra Streisand effect' by highlighting and giving further legs to the offending allegations. The truth is that the initial publication of the story on some questionable news outlet is often the least of the problems by the time it has been repeated and exaggerated all over social media.

Another example was the case of businessman and former Irish presidential candidate, Gavin Duffy, who contacted me after a concerted barrage of 'dark ads' came to his attention. The ads stated that he was involved in a cryptocurrency scheme from which he had made a fortune, that he was now endorsing the scheme to the general public, and that this endorsement had caused him to fall out of favour with the Irish political and financial authorities. Being a very successful businessman and entrepreneur, the adverse ramifications for him were obvious and far-reaching, and were compounded by paid-for-posts on Facebook stating that he was recently deceased. As in the many similar cases I have had to deal with in recent times, these false postings travel like wildfire and are incredibly difficult to terminate without the active participation of the social media platform.

Thanks to Miriam O'Callaghan's determination, Facebook, since her case, have introduced a specific reporting tool which has been of assistance in the short term, but in the greater scale of things, with the advent of AI, we could be back to square one very soon. However, not many people would have the tenacity and resolve to take on these powerful platforms. For Miriam, it involved several years of sometimes groundbreaking and stressful litigation, not only in challenging Facebook, but also in exposing the identities of those behind the fraudulent ads with the assistance of an order of the High Court in Ireland.

Fortunately, we were able to put a stop to these particular incidences of online trolling, but dealing with each case on an ad hoc basis produces differing reactions from social media companies, which is likely to remain the case until effective legislation is introduced.

This brings us back to the often insurmountable hurdle of the exorbitant cost of taking action against the likes of Google/YouTube in each jurisdiction where the disinformation has been circulated. We have received costs estimates from the lawyers acting for wealthy individual defendants of almost £3 million in one particular defamation case in London, and this is without taking into account the plaintiff's own legal fees. It was also for just one jurisdiction. This is but one example illustrating the unpredictable financial risks involved, particularly if the offending video or allegations have been published worldwide. Indeed, the actor Hugh Grant recently indicated that he felt he had no alternative but to settle with the publisher of a tabloid in a phone hacking case to avoid the risk of a total legal costs bill amounting to £10 million.

Another problem people face when they have been the subject of disinformation or even a negative media report is that they are perceived as a wounded animal, and it can become open season on them. While this may be justified in some cases, in others it can lead to a devastating and unfair indictment, undermining the basic legal principle that everyone is presumed innocent until proven guilty. Prince Andrew is probably the most obvious example, at least in terms of the speed and intensity of the public onslaught against him from the outset of the controversy.

Although not directly related to sanctions or misinformation, serious consequences can also follow when someone is classified as a Politically Exposed Person (PEP). This status means that financial institutions and employers must undertake additional and often onerous due diligence on the person concerned, with further reputational implications. The impact of PEP status has even more far-reaching repercussions than were possibly originally intended as a result of the broad definition used in the assessment of the status and the onus placed on financial institutions. These institutions leave nothing to chance, not least due to the enormous fines imposed on a number of the international banks for breaches of money laundering regulations. The definition can also encompass a very wide group of loosely connected people, who are for example linked by family ties or related by marriage or association. The widely reported closure of Brexit campaigner Nigel Farage's account at Coutts bank in

June 2023 is a possible example of the consequences of being classified as a PEP, although there has been some confusion about the precise reasons why his account was closed.

There is almost a paranoia surrounding any large transaction emanating from an overseas source. This attitude has come about as a consequence of the banks' own failings, and the fines and censorship they have received, with the customer having to pay the price at the end of the day. As a result, many successful entrepreneurs are being forced to utilise other banking facilities provided by a string of new online and start-up financial operations. Whether this turns out to be a positive development remains to be seen.

Of course, none of these factors are likely to have any adverse impact on the banking sector, which continues to profit with impunity regardless of past indiscretions or failings. It is the individual account holder who usually bears the brunt of whatever interventions may be regarded as appropriate at any given time. Sensitivity on the part of many financial institutions has often been capitalised on by political and commercial opponents around the world, in the knowledge that one simple adverse reference to some form of alleged criminality, in whatever obtuse media or online source, will inevitably be picked up by a person's bank. The reaction can range from a temporary refusal to allow a transfer of funds to the ultimate penalty of a total suspension of the account. The holder can then face a very difficult challenge in trying to persuade another bank to provide a replacement facility. An additional difficulty that international banking customers face is suspicions about financial transactions solely based on where the money is coming from. I have been consulted by a number of clients whose accounts have been arbitrarily closed, regardless of the size of their bank balance. One suffered this fate because he had sought to transfer £1 million from Bangkok to his London bank account, even though he had no difficulty in establishing the legitimacy and source of the funds.

A fundamental factor is that any disinformation is very often accessible on search engine and social media platforms, which would not have been the case fifteen or twenty years ago. The platforms will often only comply and co-operate with a formal court order, which in turn can take months to obtain, so the vast majority of victims are left to fend for themselves in an impossible situation.

On the one hand, Google, Meta and X/Twitter will argue differing degrees of freedom of speech as their mantra, but this argument is often incompatible with the rights, and sometimes the very survival, of people exposed to online attacks. Also gone are the days when I could make a call to an experienced editor, or at least a real person, who could review and consider the facts. In stark contrast, the social media companies dictate that any complaints must be channelled through their own structure of 'reporting tools' manned by unidentified persons, if they are in fact people as opposed to some form of artificial intelligence.

Bot-generated activity on X/Twitter has been the subject of a number of studies, some of which have concluded that almost 50 per cent of accounts tweeting about Covid-19 were likely to have been bots. I shudder to think of the potentially far-reaching consequences if AI had taken hold several years ago, and the negative impact of giving these bots even more capability to disseminate their disinformation more widely and effectively.

Under the Digital Services Act 2024, Big Tech will be required to take action on deepfakes and fake accounts or risk facing enormous fines. The Act requires 'expeditious removal' of material that promotes hate speech, terrorism, discrimination, or child sexual content (amongst others). Deepfakes are videos using a person's likeness to portray them doing something they never did. Platforms may be fined up to 6 per cent of their global turnover if they fail to comply. The objective behind this legislation is to discourage the platforms from gaining financial benefit from disinformation and fake news as well as increasing awareness/transparency around political advertising and curbing the spread of bots and other fake accounts. Deepfakes have been identified as an emerging form of disinformation when utilised maliciously to target politicians, celebrities and the man in the street. In recent years they have become increasingly associated with pornography with people's faces mapped onto sexually explicit material. Perhaps the best-known victim of deepfakes is the singer Taylor Swift, after artificial intelligence generated sexually explicit images of her, which flooded the internet. Taylor Swift's profile and influence is such that the White House immediately called on Congress to take legislative action to combat the increased circulation of fake explicit images.

With the increasing availability of new and more imaginative tools and apps, the difficulty of distinguishing deepfakes from real reporting is likely to become even more difficult in the years to come. Further confusion is likely to come about when genuine footage is dismissed as fake news or deepfakes by those seeking to avoid accountability. Although in recent years Big Tech companies have made efforts to detect and counter deepfakes, their general mantra has been that it is impossible to police everything, such is the volume of the information disseminated on these platforms.

The obvious conclusion is that if the Big Tech companies are unable to pinpoint and deal with disinformation, then it is unlikely that the banks will be prepared to undertake the necessary investigations to do their job for them. The banks will continue to act unilaterally if allegations such as money laundering appear on any online publication, regardless of the merits. A more difficult, and perhaps sinister, fallout from disinformation, or what can sometimes be a distortion of a person's actions, is the way the banks review press coverage and then use it as a basis on which to make decisions, regardless of its source. Some clients have been the subject of calculated references in often obscure online publications to alleged 'money laundering', a phrase about which the banks are particularly sensitive, not least due to their own past failings which have resulted in very heavy fines being imposed on them.

* * *

A client, an extremely wealthy and successful European businessman, has been targeted on account of limited contact he had with the Russian President many years earlier, which had morphed into a totally inaccurate and unfounded inference that that association still exists, and as a result, with the financial institutions again taking no chances, this client has had several of his accounts suspended for no justifiable reason, while the relevant media reports have continued to be the subject of vigorous challenge.

Just as drones have transformed the modern military battlefield, banks and bots are the new hazards in the international game of financial chess. It is no longer merely a case of how much you have at your disposal; the challenge now will be to find, and keep, a safe sanctuary for your funds. It is no wonder that the price of gold goes through the roof in times of war and controversy!

ELEVEN

Global Clients, Global Threats

Although the international element of my practice began in California, the proliferation of disinformation on internet platforms has attracted clients from all over the world – including the Middle East, Africa, Europe and South America.

Indeed, while racking my memory for interesting anecdotes to include in this book, I had almost forgotten about acting for the President of Djibouti, a wealthy Zambian family, various Libyans and Ribal al-Assad, an outspoken critic of his cousin's regime in Syria.

As my practice grew, my media profile was then sufficient to encourage influential individuals in the UK and Ireland to invite me to social events and speaking engagements, or to meet a friend who had got into trouble and whom I could perhaps help in terms of reputation or crisis management. It was through these contacts that I began to develop professional and indeed personal relationships with interesting entrepreneurs and politicians from North Africa, the Middle East and other parts of Europe. My linguistic failings continued to be a significant handicap, but one for which I tried to compensate by doing a good job of providing advice that clients could relate to and understand. Of course, the fact that most of the Big Tech companies had established their European, Middle Eastern and African headquarters in Dublin made these challenges that bit easier – I could at least get on to the litigation pitch and argue jurisdiction.

I also believe the fact that I have never been either religious or political assisted me in earning the trust of those clients who came to me, which in turn enabled me to maintain my principled stance of accepting instructions based on the merits and 'winability' of a case, as opposed to being selectively based on the potential client's personal beliefs, whatever they may be. This has resulted in me acting for Israelis and Palestinians, Russians and Ukrainians, Libyans from both sides of their extremely complex geographical divide, and senior figures from various parts of Africa and the Middle East. Although there are often language barriers between us, the similarity of the issues facing these people from various parts of the world arising from inflammatory content on YouTube, Facebook, TikTok, Instagram and Twitter/X provides common ground, and means I have an understanding of the client's concerns. Nonetheless there have been many challenges in interpreting detail, never mind local subtleties and customs.

I have had to accept the limits of my language-learning capabilities, and I continue to hope that my Northern Irish accent will not present too many additional problems, while disciplining myself to speak much more slowly than usual. One Middle Eastern client remarked that he thought he could understand English until he heard me speaking! In the meantime, my wife and partner in our law firm, Selena Tweed, has been utilising her multilingual talents and is gradually adding Arabic to her repertoire. In this global era, it is a given that language skills are a significant advantage for any young lawyer hoping to develop a career in international media law, with French, Arabic and Spanish (in that order), being the most commonly used languages after English, at least in my world. This is the future, and hopefully the next generation of lawyers will be able to avoid the embarrassment and frustration I have suffered as a result of my own limitations!

The need for languages has been a relatively new challenge for me, but one thing that has not changed at all over the forty plus years of my career is the importance of maintaining complete impartiality, and that I am seen to be impartial and independent. Some recent events have threatened everything that I have worked for and have come about as a result of a targeted disinformation campaign.

I was deeply concerned when I was made aware through documentation passed on by a respected US journalist in 2023 that an investigation company had targeted me at the behest of a state with a perceived grievance towards me, for whatever reason, this being part of a disinformation campaign. The material that was passed to me was loaded with misinformation, opening with the absurd – and provably untrue – allegation that my law firm had been financed by the United Arab Emirates (UAE). The intention had been to put false or distorted information out there in an attempt to undermine my professional integrity and independence. This revelation at least provided me with my own personal experience of being the target of disinformation at first hand, even though the threatened campaign has not, to the best of my knowledge, been implemented. It also gave me a taste of what was to come, and how faction – in other words, the mixing of facts and fiction – can be utilised very cleverly to give credibility to disinformation, and make it very difficult to counter or have removed.

The early stages of the conspiracy going on behind the scenes had not only been apparent from the aforesaid 'strategy' document, but the extent of the investigation company's influence was also revealed by the number of offices they had, from Washington to New York and London.

Furthermore, having spent a professional lifetime detecting and taking action in relation to breaches of my clients' privacy and data, I had been taken aback to read an article in *The Sunday Times* on 5 November 2022 edition headlined 'Exposed: The global hacking network that targets VIPs'. It claimed that my email account – along with the emails of a number of my clients – might have been unlawfully accessed, because of my client's perceived negativity to Qatar and, in particular, their conduct during the World Cup bidding process. A whistle-blower had apparently provided extensive information relating to the hacking of the emails of high-profile people, including the Prime Minister of Switzerland, a French senator, a British politician and a German lawyer.

I had always worked on the basis, or at least hoped, that as an officer of the court I would be immune from this kind of attack, and also that I was protected by my firm's robust cyber security measures. The ease with which the Indian-based hackers claimed that they had been able to infiltrate IT systems, however sophisticated, was very worrying. The fact that it was confirmed that my firm's IT team had been able to thwart this attempt to access my emails was only of limited comfort: I was alert to the risk that more could follow and that this may only have been the tip of the iceberg. I was also aware that two of the clients named in the article, Ghanem Nuseibeh and Mark Somos, had been victims of hacking attempts in the past, and that their data had been accessed and also distorted in order to undermine and embarrass them.

It perhaps had come as no surprise that Ghanem Nuseibeh, the Chairman of Cornerstone Global Associates, had been a target due to his reports referencing corruption relating to Qatar and their World Cup bid. A concealed listening device had been discovered at his London office; he also had reason to believe that his mailbox had been accessed and that he had been followed. Ghanem firmly believed that whoever was behind these attempts had been not only seeking information, but also to trying intimidate and harass him because of his outspoken views. The fact that *The Sunday Times* journalist Jonathan Calvert, who also apparently had his own emails hacked, had authored a book on corruption surrounding the FIFA World Cup bid and had written several negative stories for *The Sunday Times* about Qatar's conduct during the bidding process, tended also to point the finger of suspicion at that country.

Although I have always been extremely cautious in the information that I send on our office email account, in recent times I have also decided that I shouldn't send anything that I, or my clients, wouldn't be comfortable to see on the front page of a national newspaper or on social media.

A forewarning had come in an article published in *The New York Times* on 1 February 2019 based on 'several batches of documents from an anonymous source' containing what my client complained were a mix of commentary, inaccuracies and distorted 'facts'. It led me to write formally to the newspaper's legal department on behalf of Ghanem Nuseibeh and his consulting firm. To be fair to *The New York Times* lawyer, he had taken the complaint very seriously and had arranged for certain, albeit limited amendments. However, the article remained potentially damaging because of the doubt created by what appeared to be a toxic combination of distorted facts and misleading information in the aforesaid documents, which gave an aura of credibility, further enhanced by the global reputation of *The New York Times*. Although some of these matters were ultimately resolved, the experience provided an unnerving illustration of the behind-the-scenes subterfuge taking place across the world, utilising a combination of misinformation, media stories and cyber-attacks.

The problem is that although the hacking of emails is deemed unlawful in most civilised countries, it is still practised by or on behalf of some governments and is extremely difficult to detect, never mind prevent. This means that we are facing a threat that is becoming increasingly common but virtually impossible to control.

Although the harassment of one of my clients has been the subject of complaints to the police, with the Met's anti-terrorist team becoming involved at one point, law enforcement authorities have limited resources available to them. Although many of these unlawful actions are taking place on national soil, the perpetrators tend to operate from corporate entities based outside the jurisdiction where the offending activities are taking place.

In May 2023 Georgetown University Press published a book entitled *Subversion: The Strategic Weaponization of Narratives* by Dr Andreas Krieg. In the book, I was accused of intimidating targets to silence criticism of the UAE. Although the author avoided using my name in the relevant section, he made reference to several media articles which left no doubt as to my identity. It clearly didn't matter to him that none of the articles he cited actually supported his defamatory description of me and my work: he nonetheless sought to portray me as a subversive agent of the UAE, who would stoop to unethical and unprofessional tactics.

Another assault on my professional integrity came following a series of questions I received from a Beirut-based media operation, Daraj, referring to work I had undertaken for a respected UAE aeronautical-engineer and artist, Ms Maryam Al Balooshi, inferring that I had acted improperly and with an ulterior motive. The questions from Daraj – emanating from a general email address and not from a named journalist – were stated to be on behalf of a European consortium of media outlets and had been based on selective and distorted extracts from hacked emails and other communications.

The work I had undertaken on behalf of the aeronautical engineer came about because Al Jazeera had initially published an article, using her photograph and stating that she was imprisoned in Dubai and was being subjected to torture. She had never been imprisoned in her life, and naturally, I worked to get this erroneous material taken down as quickly and effectively as possible. However, the questions from Daraj implied that I had been acting improperly and in breach of professional ethics.

Information was distorted in order to create the false impression that in seeking the removal of articles carrying the engineer/artist's photograph and name, and which wrongly claimed that she was a prisoner in Dubai, I had really been seeking to remove reports of a prisoner of a similar name at the behest of the UAE. The article conveniently did not mention the significance of the photograph being published in the first place by Al Jazeera, the Qatari-owned broadcaster, which promptly removed the photo and references to my client when challenged by my firm. No explanation was offered as to how such a blatant 'mistake' could have arisen in the first place. In the meantime, the photographs and reference to my client were picked up by other media outlets and of course a number of the social media platforms, causing great distress and frustration to her, not helped by the delay in their removal.

Subsequently, the publication of misleading articles in a French outlet, *Mediapart*, and in other media outlets from Spain to Switzerland, sought to portray another totally misleading, distorted and false impression of my work. Selective extracts from a client's hacked emails were then published on a platform entitled *Abu Dhabi Secrets*, which also included highly sensitive information about a client of Dr Mark Somos creating a potential threat to life, but which, to be fair to the hosts of the platform, WordPress, was taken down immediately upon receipt of our formal complaint on behalf of our client.

It will ultimately be for the courts to assess and determine the issues arising from these attacks on my reputation. What happened to me highlights the extent adversaries will go to in order to spread disinformation on a global scale. If an experienced media lawyer like me can fall prey to such tactics, then the general public certainly need to be on their guard.

I am not holding out any hope of support or assistance from the UK government. During the course of representing a client in the thick of what turned out to be a vicious dispute between the Qatari owners of the Maybourne Hotel Group, which includes Claridge's, my firm submitted Freedom of Information requests pertaining to the diplomatic status of a former Qatari prime minister. When we thought we had the Foreign Office pinned down, we were then met with a blunt indication that no further information would be forthcoming. This refusal was stated to be due to the UK wishing to maintain 'trust and confidence' and 'its ability to protect and promote UK interests through international relations' which would be 'hampered, which will not be in the public interest'. I think this says everything!

Ukraine described their country as facing the first hybrid war – that they are fighting a battle in a digital sphere as well as on the ground. Russian, Chinese and Middle Eastern hackers are continuously in the news, although in my own experience, most of the 'guns for hire' base themselves in India. A primary focus in recent times has been on the NSO Group and their Pegasus spyware which, although intended as a force for good to protect governmental institutions, allegedly has on occasion been hijacked by unscrupulous individuals and bodies intent on the illegal extraction of information from their targets.

Rarely a day goes by when I do not receive a warning from one of the Law Societies about a suspected cyber fraud that has been perpetuated on another member of the profession. While these incidents tend to relate to financial fraud, the most concerning attacks are those that attempt to seize data, which can be utilised for blackmail or undermining the intended target. Although most of this information will be common knowledge to many, it remains alarming to read about successful cyber-attacks of this nature taking place on a daily basis, and to which most of us remain extremely vulnerable despite all the highly publicised warnings. As to what lawyers can do to assist enforcement agencies in dealing with this global problem remains to be seen, in circumstances where, as mentioned above, the legal profession itself often falls foul of these sophisticated online attacks.

We are now in a world where we must assume that our personal communications can be accessed at the whim of anyone with a passing or strategic interest. While the constant blame games go on as to who was responsible on any given occasion, the bottom line is that we just do not, and probably will never, know the full extent of the subterfuge going on behind the scenes.

This is not to say that some good old-fashioned surveillance is no longer in play. During a family holiday to Abu Dhabi, my wife booked a sand dune experience in a 4 x 4 vehicle for the family. The booking was made at the tour desk in the lobby of the Jumeirah Resort on Saadiyat Island. We were informed at the last minute that two other people were to be picked up from another hotel. It turned out to be a two-star operation in the commercial centre of Abu Dhabi, which we thought to be a strange choice for two people on holiday. They were waiting for the vehicle outside the hotel and, as we approached, my wife remarked under her breath that the couple seemed to be a bit mismatched, but neither of us thought any more of it at the time. During the trip the man told us that he was Italian and his partner was Slovakian. She said that she had been living in London for seventeen years, which was surprising given the standard of her spoken English. I really should have been more alert to what was going on, but being on holiday, I had perhaps let my guard slip a little. At the time, I didn't take notice of the fact that the pair walked off from the tourist event that formed part of our trip to have a drink on their own but left a large shopping bag open beside us. In hindsight, this most probably contained their recording device – not that they would have heard anything that would be of any interest to them or concern to us.

A couple of days later, after we had landed at Dublin airport, I went to get the car from the car park nearby while my wife and two teenage children collected our luggage. When I came back to meet them at a café, my wife immediately pointed out, in utter astonishment, that the couple from the sand dune trip were standing in the corner. I did not believe her at first but then saw that she was right. By this stage they were waiting to collect their coffee, and I walked over to them and expressed my amazement that it was such a small world! I noticed how nervous the woman seemed to be, while the man was calm and only hesitated briefly before telling me that they were due to get a connecting flight to London later that day. Given that our flight left Abu Dhabi in the early hours of the morning and that there are numerous flights during daytime hours direct to London airports, I knew that their presence in Dublin had to be beyond any coincidence, not least due to them claiming when we first met them that their home was in northern Italy.

I have been given every reason to believe that this couple were private investigators paid to follow and presumably intimidate us. While my wife and I are hardened lawyers, we were very concerned that our teenagers were exposed to this type of conduct. I immediately filed a report with the Gardaí and a complaint to the United Nations Special Rapporteur on the Independence of Judges and Lawyers.

I have been subjected to similar surveillance while working in London and abroad, and have become accustomed, if not immune, to this nonsense – although it tends to freak out any friends or colleagues who happen to be with me at the time. Given what I have been exposed to in earlier years during the Troubles in Northern Ireland, it hasn't caused me to lose any sleep. Not quite what should be a typical day in the life of a media lawyer, but unfortunately, this scenario is becoming increasingly part of the package you take on when entering my area of the legal profession. If privacy is like water, I am afraid that we have entered an era of worldwide drought, and it is unlikely to rain any time soon.

As my own experiences have shown, the online battlefields present organisations and countries with unprecedented opportunities to attack rival nations, political opponents and commercial competitors, and no one is immune from getting caught in the crossfire. The social media companies control their platforms, and decide who is entitled to use and remain on them. They also have the defence of 'free speech' to hide behind and with which to justify any inaction and policies. Given the exponential spread of bots and fake news, it is not hard to imagine the risk of those with ulterior motives infiltrating and influencing the online companies.

On another note, Qatar for example, has to a large extent side-stepped overt criticism, possibly due to their extensive financial interests and investments in London and other major cities worldwide. Such is their enormous property portfolio, encompassing vast swathes of prime London real estate and luxury hotels, that the guides on tourist boat trips along the River Thames point out the Tower of London and other national landmarks, along with the enormous Qatari property empire on view from the water. Saudi Arabia is perhaps not far behind in UK property ownership but cannot match the profile achieved by Qatar, with Qatar's extensive television advertising of their national airline and connections established at the heart of the government, all due to their vast wealth and expenditure in London and elsewhere. This will have provided a significant layer of protection against the tsunami of criticism the country has come under, including that emanating from the controversial circumstances surrounding their successful World Cup bid.

While physical investments and even direct lobbying are relatively overt, the fear has to be that this financial power could be directed towards achieving control or influence over the social media and search engine giants, or at least some of their policy decisions. Notwithstanding the huge impact and control that the global publishing platforms have over our daily lives, relatively little is known about their decision-making processes behind the scenes. Some Middle Eastern and European Union (EU) Member States have expressed their frustration that Google/YouTube and other Big Tech operators limit their remedial actions to the jurisdiction of the complainant rather than dealing with complaints on an international basis, a common scenario faced by many of my clients.

Although most of the major platforms confirm that they will, and they do, comply with court orders, I have to ask why they are not prepared to adopt more of an early adjudication role, and assess offending comments based on representations made to them in all appropriate cases. As I have repeatedly highlighted, the costs of having to obtain a court order in each and every jurisdiction where there is publication are both exorbitant and prohibitive for most people. Just as a newspaper editorial team has always been expected and required to police what it publishes and to act accordingly, I can find absolutely no good reason why the platforms should not have to do likewise.

One example has been particularly frustrating for myself and my client Kheir Allab, an Algerian with dual French citizenship, in other words, someone entitled to the benefit of protection under EU legislation as well as within his own national courts. He has been subjected to a relentless campaign of harassment by two people on their YouTube channels, who have displayed a personal agenda against him. In any event, although Mr Allab had obtained court judgments in his favour in Switzerland, France and Algeria, Google had been only prepared to comply with each respective order, restricted to the borders of the individual jurisdiction in each case. Mr Allab was left with the unenviable, if not impossible, challenge of having to bear the legal costs of applying to each court in every country in the world where the offending YouTube channels could be accessed. The client was concerned and frustrated that the two people harassing him may actually have been profiting from the normal commission paid by YouTube based on the number of hits on their sites. Unfortunately, Kheir Allab, in common with most of the rest of the international population, does not have the funds to take on such extensive proceedings.

Like Google, Facebook have taken it upon themselves to be their own judge and jury, and have even gone so far as to undertake their own 'jury selection'. Each member of their initial Oversight Board has been selected by Facebook themselves, leaving them vulnerable to criticism, fair or unfair, of potential bias. The fundamental principle behind jury selection in the traditional judicial system is of course to avoid such perceptions by ensuring a rigorous and transparent selection process with the involvement of the trial judge and the lawyers representing all the parties to the proceedings.

What some of the platforms do not appear to understand is that they are being judged and assessed by their actions, and not by the extensive high-profile banner advertising of their stated stance towards privacy and data protection. The public are not stupid, but unfortunately, governments, as discussed in previous chapters, appear reluctant to follow up with legislative backbone to implement the protections so desperately overdue and needed.

Some countries clandestinely fund outside firms to implement hacking and harassment, making it very difficult to link a government to a specific action. I am frequently consulted about calculated agendas implemented by state players, particularly in the Middle East, who use increasingly sophisticated tools to enhance their social media campaigns, ranging from the creation of fake news sites and random bots, and distorting the content of legitimate sites, to impersonating journalists or opposition figures. Another strategy to which a number of my clients have fallen victim, is the hacking of rivals' or opponents' private information, followed by its distortion and publication. For instance, a group called 'GlobaLeaks' disseminated emails and other hacked documents of the UAE ambassador to the United States to various US media outlets.

One interesting factor that has come to light when dealing with different parts of the world is how different countries favour different platforms for their own particular social or commercial usage. For instance, YouTube is extremely popular in North African and Middle Eastern countries, whereas Facebook comes to the

FROM HOLYWOOD TO HOLLYWOOD

fore in countries like Zambia and other parts of southern Africa. In the Middle East, WhatsApp is treated with a considerable degree of suspicion, with several nations, from time to time, blocking its use within their territorial boundaries. Although WhatsApp has always vigorously denied that their system can be accessed, there has been strong suspicion and many claims to the contrary, including from several of my own clients who have been convinced that their WhatsApp messages have been accessed by bad actors.

The communication app of choice tends to run in phases, with Proton Mail, at one point regarded as the most secure means of sending email communications, but with their invincibility being questioned as a result of some adverse publicity arising from users claiming that their Proton mails had been hacked, rightly or wrongly. Other users restrict their communications to Signal, Telegram or Threema. Each of these services appeared infallible at one point, but in each case their security has come under adverse scrutiny, and then there is a surge of users moving to another service provider until the same thing happens again. The reality is that nobody really knows how safe and secure any of these alternatives are, but such is the sensitivity, and often paranoia, of certain users that any rumour, false or otherwise, is enough to shake confidence.

Many of my clients will not communicate by email at all, insisting on face-to-face meetings or hand-delivered correspondence, which means that I have to travel frequently to the Middle East, North Africa and elsewhere. At one point during the pandemic restrictions, several clients even resorted to use of the regular postal service. During meetings all devices are switched off and left outside the room. Such is the way we have to live our professional lives in the modern era. I dread to think how all this is going to pan out for the next generation. The extent of this cyber warfare must mean that the IT systems currently available will very soon be made redundant, and it remains to be seen what type of secure means of communication will replace them.

However, the fundamental problem facing my North African and Middle Eastern clients in particular relates to the tendency of several social media platforms to bounce any complaints from that part of the world over to what is perceived as the more secure protection offered in the US. I have found this stance as frustrating as it is incredible, given that these platforms have described their operations in Dublin as their European, Middle Eastern and African headquarters. I had naively assumed that this specific geographic title would genuinely mean that any complaints should be directed there.

One example that caused me much bemusement was when Facebook and Twitter referred a complaint I had made on behalf of the Maat Group – a Cairo-based media company – to the platforms' headquarters in the US. The Maat Group's social media accounts had been suspended to their complete surprise, and they had been given no explanation as to why this had happened. Although I questioned Facebook and Twitter about this, and ridiculed them for trying to argue that Egypt was neither a Middle Eastern nor an African country, they managed to dodge the issue by asserting that our client had agreed to the US jurisdiction in their signing-on contract with the platform. Unfortunately, despite our lengthy protests, the Maat Group's accounts remained suspended. There are times when you really do feel like giving up!

A hint of what might be to come, and is actually happening, could be found in a report from a very respected internet monitoring operation, which included a subtle indication that Facebook and Twitter had been swapping notes with regard to the purported actions of certain users. The report itself, although prepared by a reputable organisation, gave the impression of having been based on information favouring the Muslim Brotherhood.

While all this may be viewed as yet another example of Big Tech protecting and suiting themselves, and moving the goalposts as and when necessary, it also presents considerable challenges for lawyers attempting to safeguard their clients from online harassment. In the meantime, these international platforms are able to select jurisdictions of *their* own choosing in order to take advantage of the most favourable tax regimes. It really would appear to be a case of one-way traffic.

TWELVE

I am Not a Robot ...

I come from an era which to me still seems not so long ago – in fact it's more than forty years past – when secretarial staff still used typewriters, first manual, then electric. On the rare occasions when I travelled abroad, I had to make arrangements to post dictation tapes back to the office to be typed up. Back then there was no expectation of speed, and a response time was given in days or even weeks. When the fax machine arrived, there was some expectation of speedier responses but – unlike its successors – it didn't raise any security or confidentiality concerns.

The phone, however, has always been vulnerable to being accessed unlawfully, and sometimes lawfully. Mo Mowlam, in her time as secretary of state for Northern Ireland, granted the security services the legal right to access certain phone lines of interest. What she didn't seem to realise at the time was that in granting this fairly broad permission, she had also unwittingly facilitated the accessing of her own phone lines. This led to some of her conversations with Martin McGuinness, then one of the Sinn Féin negotiators during the peace process, being published in the newspapers. Her referring to him as 'sweetie pie' was tabloid gold.

Subsequently, I was consulted by one of the government employees who had been tasked with administering this phone accessing. He had decided to write a book about his experiences, only to find himself the subject of a rapidly served D-notice, prohibiting any references to his work being published for reasons of national security. In any event, the notice put an end to his ambitions at that stage.

We had assumed that the fax machine could not be bettered, but how wrong could we have been? The advent and rapid development of the internet not only took the whole world by storm, but it revolutionised the way lawyers worked and presented dramatic challenges that could never have been anticipated only a few years earlier. Although the legal profession – in common, quite surprisingly, with journalists – was very slow to embrace this new, global, facility, computer screens and laptops gradually became the norm during the course of the 1990s.

Even these dramatic changes to office life were nothing in comparison to what was to come with the advent of Wi-Fi, followed by the dominance of the social media platforms. I still recall as if it was yesterday – a representative of our IT service provider telling us that Wi-Fi would never catch on! At the time, he was attempting to interest us in a 'portable' battery for a laptop, which was the size and weight of the proverbial brick, and which

I was expected to carry with me on my business travels. As the online news and social media outlets continued to expand, the traditional media declined. It would not be long before about 80 per cent of my work would be related to or as a result of online publication. Looking back, I can see more clearly the structure and inevitability of these advances across society and the gradual impact on the legal profession. Nonetheless, I don't think anything could have prepared us for the dramatic introduction of and developments in AI.

Over the years I have often complained that it is well-nigh impossible to speak to an actual human being within the social media and search engine organisations. Invariably, we are met with what seems like a robotic rejection of a client's complaint, indicating that the offending post does not breach the platform's rules and guidelines, with no other explanation or engagement forthcoming. The rapid development of online AI has created a whole new challenge, not just for media lawyers but for society in general. Attempting to negotiate with a robot, never mind reason with it, is as farcical as it is impossible. The Daleks in the original *Dr Who* television series come to mind, the irony being that we are often asked to complete an online test to establish that 'I am not a robot'!

Not only is it pointless to attempt to reason with an AI platform, but the absence of the ability to engage with a human removes a fundamental aspect of interaction between lawyers and those on the other side of the negotiating fence. The emotions, such as empathy, understanding and even fear, that can play such a crucial role in settlement discussions are removed from the negotiating process at a stroke. Mediation is currently up in the air when it comes to the AI platforms, never mind the more basic face-to-face discussions that have so often resulted in civil litigation cases being settled before reaching or at the doors of the court.

AI development continues at an unrelenting pace, with all the Big Tech companies, including Microsoft, Google and Amazon, involved in a race to develop AI systems and leverage them for maximum commercial use. However, even high-profile entrepreneurs who have been involved in the race in one way or another, such as Elon Musk, have expressed concerns about the rapid pace of development and the risks that it may pose to society. There are also extensive issues regarding data protection, copyright infringement and disinformation. The developing pace of AI also poses an increasing regulatory problem for the EU and international governments attempting to implement a legislative framework with a view to exercising some degree of regulatory control.

The cyber strategies of the modern era are increasingly sophisticated and difficult to discover. Such have been the rapid developments in satellite monitoring and cyber infiltration, I have been told that an operative can sit in an office almost anywhere in the world and listen into any conversation or intercept emails from wherever they are based. No need to utilise the more traditional method of hacking or blagging, which has been the subject of extensive litigation in the courts. The mind boggles as to the impact of AI on this type of surveillance.

Although AI is widely used for research and fun – with people using it to write jokes, poems and songs, and to support education and preparation for academic examinations – it has not taken very long for serious problems to emerge. For instance, in April 2023 ChatGPT cited a sexual harassment scandal and named an actual law professor as the accused. Not only were the allegations false, but the purported scandal was given further credibility by the platform citing a non-existent article in the *Washington Post* as the source of the information. Many other similar instances began to emerge worldwide, with each case being just as difficult to resolve. The chatbot in the first instance refused to accept that it had published falsehoods and that a mistake had been made, and it, of course, lacked any human empathy or concern. Although I am not an expert in US law, I know enough to understand that the professor would be facing a much higher threshold in terms of proving malice or recklessness to succeed in a libel claim. However, in this particular case, I would be arguing that malice was constituted in the extreme recklessness on the part of the owners of the chatbot to allow this foreseeable scenario to come about.

Another example was when another AI chatbot falsely claimed that several Irish lawyers, including a senior judge, were under investigation after being publicly accused of sexual misconduct. This came about when, to test the chatbot, an online news outlet put a similar scenario to it as the one that had been put to ChatGPT in the US, asking for a list of members of the legal profession in Ireland who had been accused of sexual misconduct. This chatbot came up with a number of names of legal professionals but none of them had in fact been accused of any such crime; it then cited a non-existent article from the very publication that had posed this question to it in the first place.

The serious consequences arising from AI-generated responses such as these cannot be overstated. It is all very well that those behind the chatbots protest that they are consistently improving their service, but this provides little comfort to those suffering potentially devastating collateral damage in the interim. Certainly, if such errors manifested on the pages of a regional newspaper, then the financial consequences could put the lights out.

All this begs the question as to whether an AI chatbot, or rather its owner, can be sued for defamation. In the US, eminent UCLA law professor Eugene Volokh convened a group of legal experts to discuss artificial intelligence and free speech, and in a subsequent article he came to the conclusion that ChatGPT, or any AI content provider, is legally liable for defamatory content subject to certain conditions. Crucially, Professor Volokh and his contemporaries took the view that Section 230 of the Communications Decency Act 1996 does not apply to AI. As mentioned earlier in this book, Section 230 currently provides legal immunity for hosting content generated by others. However, AI-generated content is different in that it is produced by the programmes themselves rather than hosting content generated by others. I would argue, and indeed will be arguing, the same logic applies to the e-comm Directive, which the online platforms have persistently sought to rely upon in Europe. Certainly, there will be much legal debate and action going forward.

Legislators in Europe in particular have been quicker to react to AI than they have been in relation to earlier instances of online harm. The European Parliament prepared a set of proposals to form part of the EU's Artificial Intelligence Act, with the aim of regulating the development and deployment of AI systems in the EU based on their level of risk to human health, safety and fundamental rights. In doing so, they also designate certain specific uses of AI as 'high-risk', binding developers to stricter requirements of transparency, safety and human oversight. However, the reality is that this law is unlikely to have an immediate impact while the AI operators continue to compete with each other in developing and expanding AI even further. The complexity and speed of the growth of ChatGPT has upended work done to date, as this type of AI, a large language model, has no single intended use and can be used for a variety of purposes, thereby making it difficult to categorise it into a specific risk category and therefore to regulate it. Somewhat predictably, EU policymakers were lobbied vigorously to exclude general-purpose AI, like ChatGPT, from the obligations imposed on high-risk AI systems.

The approach on the part of the online developers to the escalating concerns has been to call for the implementation of regulatory measures. This has been a united mantra from all the big players when appearing before congressional and other parliamentary forums. Of course, the cynic would say that such concessions have only been advanced to delay reform and buy time while they race against each other to secure commercial advantage for the long term.

One example that I believe says everything in highlighting the sometimes nonchalant attitude of many of the tech companies has been on at least one occasion Google's response to an email complaint in sending a letter *by post* as opposed to replying by email. Coming from a company that epitomises and leads the way in online communication, I personally found this somewhat frustrating.

Another key consideration is that many of the chatbots see themselves as a kind of Wikipedia on speed, offering themselves as news and factual aggregators. At the same time, the banks and other financial institutions are continuing to react to media coverage, which may very well include information from the chatbots, as a reason to suspend or close accounts or blackball a particular customer without them knowing. Political and commercial rivals have already jumped on this type of disinformation strategy as a means of causing financial havoc for their target.

Whatever the outcome of any forthcoming legislation, AI will most certainly form a central and pivotal role in our daily lives. Such has been the pace of development that the fear is that not only will these systems take on a life of their own, but the legislators and the law are likely to be left trailing hopelessly behind, with lawyers left to do battle on the front line with very little weaponry at their disposal. All the while, many of the powerful movers behind AI development continue to make pledges to harness and control development, but their promises relate to the future rather than the present time. Their public commitments to safety and transparency, and apparent willingness to establish best practices for controlling AI, are one thing, but we have heard it all before from the social media platforms.

In my opinion, unless robust legislation with teeth is put in place sooner rather than later, we are likely to see a rapid surge in harmful and potentially dangerous content, without any recourse for the ordinary person on the street. I appreciate that it is important not to discourage innovation; but it is equally important to impose regulation that can evolve. On balance, I am of the view that caution must take precedence. Self-regulation has not worked for the most part so far as many of the Big Tech platforms are concerned, and therefore there is no reason to believe that leaving it to the AI platforms to regulate themselves is any more likely to be successful.

What then does the future hold? AI is revolutionising the space sector, particularly in the areas of satellite surveillance and military communications. The vast amount of data generated by satellites can be efficiently processed and analysed by AI algorithms, enabling faster and more accurate threat detection and identification of areas of interest. On the plus side, AI will be infinitely faster and more efficient at noticing 'red flags' in data such as buzzwords or suspicious activity. On the downside, there is no evidence of appropriate training, never mind regulation. For example, if an AI satellite hears the word 'bomb', it immediately associates it with terrorism. AI would not understand that phrases such as 'there's a bomb' or 'bomb disposal squad' are acceptable. This is particularly important when AI surveillance overlaps with autonomous weapons (satellites and drones) and has the power to launch an attack.

Google was helping the Pentagon develop 'Maven', a satellite AI surveillance programme, until its workers launched a protest over growing fears of weaponised AI and all quit. In a letter they said, 'building this technology to assist the US Government in military surveillance – and potentially lethal outcomes – is not acceptable'.

Satellite surveillance is already commonly used by military and law enforcement services worldwide. Private operations are doing likewise and are making a mockery of privacy laws and protections. The phone hacking scandals even now represent a period in history when surveillance necessitated access to voicemails or computers. The vast array of satellites in outer space, increasing by the month, will be able to eavesdrop and view every aspect of a person's private life. Even the private sanctuary of the bathroom will no longer be sacrosanct, never mind the confession box or the doctor's surgery.

Whether appropriate shields can be developed remains to be seen, but certainly it is unlikely that the law can or will provide any realistic protection from bad actors determined to obtain information and data on their targeted subject.

Several years ago, the son of a good friend contacted me to enquire if I knew whether any university ran a course in space law. I had to ask him to explain what he had in mind and had to think carefully, even after he'd explained about satellites, even then, posing the greatest legal challenges for his generation. Roll on a couple of years and space law is still not appearing on many academic curriculums, suggesting that it will be quite some time before any such law is considered never mind reaches the statute books. AI was always seen as something for the future – epitomised in sci-fi and comic books – but now not only is it here, but the speed at which it has developed is extraordinary. In some ways, Big Brother from George Orwell's novel *1984* has ended up being a representation of Big Tech in 2024.

EPILOGUE

I am often asked why I still work so hard after all these years. Given the hours I have to put in just to keep ahead of the pack, I can certainly relate to the famous concert violinist who, when an audience member said to him, 'I would give my life to be able to play like you,' replied, 'Lady, that I did.'

My eldest son, Conor, decided very early on that he did not want to be a lawyer, in part because of the long hours involved in my work, which leave little time for family life, never mind anything else. He decided to enter the medical profession, ultimately specialising in respiratory and infectious diseases. Somewhat ironically as it turns out, there'd be no prizes for guessing that he has spent the last few years working gruelling long hours on the front line for the NHS, especially during the pandemic. However, he has no regrets and does a very worthwhile and critically important job. I definitely can't say the same of my career, although I do look back with profound relief at the times when a client has told me that I have saved them from taking their own life by stopping a particularly damaging false story.

In the successful practice of media law there is no room for half measures or, in my case, semi-retirement. It is all or nothing. Each case is a fight to the death unless a compromise can be reached early on. It's not a job which allows me to switch on and off as and when I feel the need for a break or even a glass of wine, out of concern that the latter may impact on a crucial judgement call. Much of the work does not come down to legal expertise or academic ability, but rather to the two core qualities that a media lawyer needs: judgement and backbone. I also can't take my eye off the objective or – of course – the opposition.

I sometimes think back to my first day in the office as a newly qualified solicitor, on that grand salary of £2,500, with my seemingly insurmountable bank overdraft of over £13,000, when I had absolutely no idea where I was going, or even whether I actually wanted to be there at all. Fast forward a few years to my unexpected involvement in the 'Cream Bun' case closely followed by the Eastwood litigation, and everything changed. Not only did these cases ignite a lifelong interest in media law, but they also exposed me to the adrenaline rush I have been chasing ever since.

As it turned out, the world of boxing isn't a million miles away from the world of media law. There's a similar pressure cooker intensity, although with less risk of physical injury. If you don't strike quickly and effectively against your opponent, they'll strike quickly and effectively against you. Just like the fight arena, the libel courts are no place for the faint-hearted. The preparations are just as important and the stakes almost as high, although the lawyer hopefully has the prospect of a longer and healthier, career.

I feel honoured to have had the privilege of working for and with many charismatic characters and astute minds, with their own unique and individual talents, ranging from prominent High Court judges (including several from the UK Supreme Court) and other lawyers to global entrepreneurs and property developers, not forgetting sports, musical and acting talent from across the world. All of them have contributed to whatever success I may have achieved over the decades. In particular, I have noticed that many of the most impressive businesspeople I have represented share the feature of paying great attention to detail – an example that I have tried to follow.

The world is changing dramatically and at an un-precedented speed, with the tech giants in the vanguard. As was graphically illustrated by the sudden demise and redundancy of the Blackberry, the public will ultimately determine the devices that will take the lead for the next generation of users. There is likely to be much more competition in the marketplace, there will be further scandals, and the pressure will be on Big Tech to maintain their grasp on the social needs and interests of their users. One thing is certain: in the short term at least, it will take much more than selective, sporadic legislation and the intervention of the courts to control and police these Big Brothers, and I most certainly do not intend to stand back and accept what appears to be an inevitable outcome in the modern era. Although these new media giants are much more difficult adversaries – not least because they make it almost impossible to communicate with a person – I relish the challenge and am determined to do everything I can to make sure they are brought to account.

At this stage of my career, I wonder whether I will have achieved anything worth mentioning. Often, at the end of a busy week, I reflect on what I have actually done, notwithstanding the cut-and-thrust engagements that form almost all of my professional working day. I have a distinct advantage in that I have always loved the work I do and have never had a shred of regret about my chosen career, even during those 3 a.m. sweats in the night when I have felt up against it with no immediate solution in sight. I have always enjoyed the hunt. Just as my late mother had a lifelong love of crossword puzzles, I relish finding solutions for clients' problems from among the options available to them.

I am still driven and perhaps over-motivated by anyone telling me that I have no chance of pulling a legal rabbit out of the hat for a particular issue. I do not believe that any scenario is insoluble, regardless of whether the solution may be limited by financial and other factors. Even as I write this, I feel that I have at least one major litigation challenge left in me.

Some years ago, I put a proposal to the respective health ministers for Northern Ireland, the Republic of Ireland, and England/Wales suggesting taking legal action against Big Tobacco, with a view to recovering at least some proportion of the multimillions spent in caring for victims of smoking, who needed treatment for emphysema, lung cancer and many other health issues. I had put together a fee structure comprising a combination of third-party funding, after-the-event insurance and no-win, no-fee arrangements that would be appropriate for each jurisdiction. Although I received some limited interest and encouragement, there wasn't enough momentum to get legal proceedings off the ground, primarily – I suspect – because of fear of the powerful tobacco companies. I sense a similar reluctance from governments to legislate against Big Tech in the current times, in spite of the proven addiction and harm users face. If governments do not have the resolve to take action themselves, then I am sure a similar funding arrangement would be available to groups of individuals, especially as more and more evidence of harm emerges.

In the same way that I was motivated to try to take on Big Tobacco as a result of watching my mother, a lifelong smoker, slowly dying of emphysema, so I would now like to take action against Big Tech as I look with consternation at the generation to which my younger children belong, which would appear to be totally addicted to screens and potentially becoming 'radicalised' by online violence and pornography. Perhaps that will be my future challenge. I am keeping all my options open.

The tide is turning against generative AI and social media platforms and search engines, which are now being held more accountable. This is not least because a number of their executives are being hauled before congressional hearings and the courts, and identified by concerned whistle-blowers from within their own ranks, exposing attitudes and conduct that we had all suspected to be going on behind the scenes. It has nonetheless been shocking to discover the scale of what's been happening, and the apparent knowledge of it within the management structure.

Of course it is similar Big Tech players who own or are developing the AI platforms while continuing to argue that they are not the publisher and therefore not responsible for the content on their sites, no matter how outrageous or defamatory. Of equal concern has been Big Tech's approach of expressing concern and voicing the need for regulation *in the future* when the rapid and uncontrolled advances in AI are a serious problem *today*. It is very easy to put this issue on the long finger to be dealt with at some indeterminate date, which in itself distracts from the need to act now. This approach appears to suit many governments, anxious to avoid direct confrontation with Big Tech and jeopardising the financial benefits to their economies.

Perhaps it will only be a matter of time before lawyers themselves succumb to the advances in AI, and the robots will not only form the judge and jury but also the legal representation itself. While many would no doubt welcome the demise of lawyers, hopefully there will be somebody out there who will still call Paul!

As I was coming to the end of writing this book at a rented holiday house in France, a rickety van with high wheel axles was parked at the bottom of the driveway. One of our party saw that an occupant of the vehicle was wearing fairly high-tech headphones and using a broadcast-standard camera which was totally out of keeping with the state of his vehicle; he seemed to be filming our comings and goings from his position underneath the van. We had some craic at mealtimes, assuming that our conversations were being listened to, making references to various types of subterfuge and chatting about matters that we knew would be of interest to his masters.

The rapid developments in cyber surveillance and in particular the role of satellites in listening to and observing every aspect of our private lives on a whim will make my experiences of being watched quaint, if not laughable. I can only hope that the next generation of lawyers will be able to master space and cyber laws to a sufficient degree in order to bring about some level of practical regulation, or at least a limited deterrent.